THE AUTHENTIC LEADER AS SERVANT (ALS)

ALS II COURSE 2
COURAGE LEADERSHIP
Attributes, Principles, and Practices

SYLVANUS N. WOSU, Ph.D.

THE AUTHENTIC LEADER AS SERVANT
ALS II COURSE 2
Developing Courage Leadership Attributes, Principles, and Practices

© Copyright 2024 by Sylvanus N. Wosu Ph.D.

Printed in the United States of America
ISBN: 978-1-7367638-7-2

All rights reserved. No part of this book may be reproduced or transmitted in any form or by any means, electronic or mechanical, including photocopying, recording, or by any information storage and retrieval system, without permission in writing from the copyright owner.

Bible quotations are from the New King James (NKJV) version of the Bible unless otherwise indicated.

Other versions used in this book are the New International Version (NIV), New Living Translation (NLT), King James Version (KJV), English Standard Version (ESV), and Good News Translation (GNT). Unless otherwise specified, NKJV should be assumed.

The views expressed in this work are solely those of the author and do not necessarily reflect the views of the publisher, and the publisher disclaims any responsibility for them.

To order additional copies of this book, contact:
Proisle Publishing Services LLC
39-67 58th Street, 1st floor
Woodside, NY 11377, USA
Phone: (+1 646-480-0129)
info@proislepublishing.com

Table of Contents

FOREWORD	XI
ACKNOWLEDGMENTS	XV
DEDICATION	XVII
PREFACE	19
About Leader As Servant Leadership (LSL) Model	22
About the Authentic Leader as Servant (ALS)	25
About the ALS Courses	26
CHAPTER 1	
UNDERSTANDING LEADERSHIP ATTRIBUTES	35
Functional Definitions	35
Comparisons With Other Works	40
Principle of Leadership Attribute	42
Authentic Leadership Attributes	43
Summary 1 Understanding Leadership Process	48
CHAPTER 2	
COURAGE LEADERSHIP ATTRIBUTE	51
Servant Leadership Courage Attribute	52
Principle of Leadership Courage Attribute	56
Learning to be Courageous	58
Summary 2 Courage Leadership Attribute	59
CHAPTER 3	
DEVELOPING COURAGE–BRAVERY	63
Inner Strength Promises to Overcome Fear	66
Case of Bravery against Fear	69
Summary 3 Developing Courage–Bravery Attribute	71
CHAPTER 4	
DEVELOPING COURAGE–STRENGTH	73
Develop a sense of inner strength	73
Develop strength from God's promises	74
Develop inner strength to sustain courage	74
Walk with God to develop spiritual strength	76
Summary 4 Developing COurage–Strength	77

CHAPTER 5
DEVELOPING COURAGE– SELF-WILL   79
Summary 5 Developing Courage–Self-Will ----- 81

CHAPTER 6
DEVELOPING COURAGE–DECISIVENESS   83
Develop a sense of quickness to act on issues ----- 83
Develop boldness to confront issues ----- 84
A Case Study of Courage for Good Success ----- 85
Bravery Model for Good Success ----- 91
The Formula for Good Success ----- 92
Summary 6 Developing Courage–decisiveness ----- 103

TOPIC INDEX   107
REFERENCES   109

Foreword

The modern world today is obsessed with standardization and modalities. As a result, in the realm of leadership, many books have spout associated leadership theories and models and explain them as the path to follow. However, the critical dimensions that distinguish the effectiveness of any leadership process are the values and attribute the leader brings to the table; desired change is influenced by leadership styles or standards. These many standards and theories of leadership often are not in step with the changing times or the followers' needs. The trend is a bit like stocking different kinds of foods in a grocery store and expecting that they will meet everybody's needs the same way and at all times. Aisles are packed with varieties of food with expiration dates in the future, but getting the best deal on the products is what really matters to those who buy and use the products

In many ways, this is the state of leadership in the modern world. Increasingly, even leaders of public institutions are tasked with turning a profit for themselves or the organization they serve. The idea of a "leader" seems to float uneasily alongside the ranks of fundraisers or profit raisers in contrast to any kind of role model for followers or employees. That which is knowable, measurable, and marketable has surpassed the difficult intangibility of strong moral leadership attributes as the central guideline for achievement and success.

In this complicated space, Dr. Sylvanus Wosu introduces his complex idea of the Leader as a Servant Leadership, which is in this book, modeled on Christian tradition. Like all intricate ideas, Dr. Wosu's central point depends on a paradox: a person is best qualified to lead when he or she is most ready to serve. This paradox has been monopolized rhetorically by "public servants" who often serve either self-interest or the interests of specific lobbies. The Authentic Leader as Servant penetrates past the superficial concept of "serving" and details the internal state of true servitude or Servanthood.

While the book is primarily focused on the Christian model of leadership attributes such as discipleship, empathy, affection, and Servanthood, it does so not merely on the grounds of blind faith, but rather via numerous contemporary sociological and business-driven studies on how leaders should seek a leader-follower relationship that is simultaneously productive and nurturing. Dr. Wosu's most piercing insights always involve this secular–Christian dialogue. This book demonstrates that Christ's model for leadership is one that may exist successfully outside the confines of a faith relationship; it places the values of Christ's religious significance in leadership at the center of the framework. It is clear from Dr. Wosu's generous own life story of faith—a faith tested by humbling difficulties—is at the center of both his orientation and motivation for writing.

In language that is so concise, it is often illustrated in mathematical formulas; Dr. Wosu explains the deep structural integrity of Christ's Leader as the Servant Leadership model. One could imagine leaders of any doctrine benefiting from the analyses contained in these pages. The book's message repeatedly encourages the reader to imagine a scenario or reflect on memories and personal experiences to prove or test its many points. Thus, the book depends on a form of praxis, a lesson that could be or has been enacted, by the participating reader. I am very impressed at the volume and level of thinking of the author. Parts of the book involve his personal story, which is especially riveting. I cannot imagine what he had to endure, which he referred to as a" wilderness walk," to accomplish the goal he set for himself. His life stories on these pages are inspiring and stimulating.

In this way, the text eschews dogmatism in favor of the self-discovery Socratic Method of teaching and learning. The reader is not badgered into complying with a religious objective but is rather asked to consider the applicability of difficult biblical concepts in relation to modern life. It is a fascinating and very thought-provoking read.

Hence, the book does not seek to make the leader a servant, a cookie-cutter corporate buzzword, but rather asks the reader to imagine him or herself interacting with a range of concepts. One of Dr. Wosu's great strengths is his reservation when it comes to forcing his reading's interpretation on the material he presents.

The book parallels Biblical and modern leadership scenarios in ways that consistently provoke thought, and while it is clear Dr. Wosu has his particular leadership style; the space for the reader's own thoughts is always left open.

The book could not have been written in any other way with integrity. Its format and formulas are offered to the reader of the leader as a servant role that it analyzes in its pages. To find a text that instructs from this humble position is profoundly refreshing in a genre that is often packaged inside a cover with a sizeable picture of the "modest" author, smiling egotistically beneath a name spelled out in large, gold lettering. Throughout its pages, this text feels as if it serves the reader.

In the end, this is the most satisfying aspect of the book. There is no standardized approach to achieving successful leadership. There is no promise of power and a bigger payday; in fact, the book often proffers just the opposite. The reader is not encouraged to devalue the experience of leadership by finding some economic metric for marking success but is rather asked to think deeply about the most basic elements of internal and social interaction within the framework of a Christian tradition. What this means will be different for every reader. Indeed, even in the context of single chapters, I found myself questioning or re-evaluating moments of my own life. This book serves; it doesn't feel like filling in multiple-choice questions, staring at a wall of flavorless grocery products, or hearing the endless servant promises of today's political scene. It feels like a humble invitation to consider a single paradoxical element of a profoundly productive tradition.

-Tobias Bates

ACKNOWLEDGMENTS

A book on leadership attributes as aspects of Servant Leadership sprouted from the wealth of knowledge and the inspirations of many other leaders. Their writings were sources of inspiration, challenges, and examples of excellence to emulate. I acknowledge the leaders listed below for their help in one way or the other. I am very grateful and I hereby express my appreciation and thanks:

Mr. Wayne Holt, introduced me first to the subject of Servanthood in one of our Stephen Ministerial Training classes, and he is the one who has conducted his life as a leader–servant; he encouraged me throughout my writing;

Dr. Harvey Borovetz, Distinguished Professor and Chair of the Bioengineering Department, is a leader-servant in many ways, he modeled Servanthood and encouragement attributes throughout his leadership in an academic setting.

Dr. Clifford and Dr. Patience Obih, in so many measures exemplified the practical leadership attributes discussed in this book.

Pastor Lance Lecocq, Lead Pastor of Monroeville Assembly of God, for his excellent model of servanthood, empowerment, and emulation attributes to the ministerial team, I am thankful for his motivation and encouragement throughout the several hours on this project;

To my administrative assistant, Ms. Terri Cook, who was always the first to review the manuscript; I am very grateful for her dedication.

To the African Christian Fellowship USA, institutions, and all other organizations where I have served in one leadership capacity or the other, thank you for affording me senior leadership positions that provided the leadership platform and opportunities to grow as a leader.

Dr. Lawrence Owoputi, a brother I am proud to call my friend; for his dedication to serving others, his generosity, healing care, and responsibility attributes during our term in office and in chapter leadership positions; he taught me that excellent following is also part of good leadership;

To Tobias Bates, for his editorial work on the original draft of the book, and his dedication to completing the work.

Mr. Edward F. Kondis, a member of our Engineering Board of Visitors, for his always encouraging and moral support;

Dr. Enefaa N. Wosu, my wife and life partner, for her love, commitment, and prayer support, especially during those long night hours I was not there for her and her constant reminder of who I must be as a leader-servant. Without her support, forbearance, wisdom, and encouragement, this project would not have been completed; I say, thank you very much.

And to God alone be all the glory and honor for the divine inspiration and guidance in initiating and completing this life-transforming book project.

DEDICATION

I humbly submit this book back unto the gracious hands of God who inspired the writings through His Holy Spirit!

I dedicate this book to my virtuous wife of 45 years, Rev. (Dr.) Enefaa Wosu whose spiritual leadership is an important gateway to our home, and to our four wonderful children—Prof. Eliada Wosu-Griffin EL, HeCareth, Tamuno-Emi, and Chidinma. From them all, I learnt what it meant to be a leader-servant. I could not be blessed with better teachers.

PREFACE

What characteristics did Biblical leaders like the Apostle Paul, Moses, Joshua, and Nehemiah as servants of their people display outwardly that distinguished them from other leaders, both then and now? The Apostle Paul kept his focus to *emulate* Christ and endured all the infirmities and persecutions he suffered to complete his goal to preach the gospel of Jesus Christ. He inspired Timothy and others through his effective *discipleship* leadership to imitate him as he emulated Christ. Moses' outward display of his *trus*t in God's power earned him a good level of trust from the people and empowered him for the mission of delivery of God's children from bondage in Egypt; he had to *reproduce* himself in Joshua to complete the mission. But the greatest of them was Jesus Christ, who humbly sacrificed His life to finish the work of redemption. In His *Servanthood*, commitment, and love for the people, He became the ultimate *model* of a leader as a servant to *emulate*.

Let's consider for a moment secular leaders in these current times! For example, think of Henry Ford, who founded the successful Ford Motor Company; Bill Gates who created the global empire that is Microsoft; Albert Einstein, who in many ways is synonymous with a genius for his contributions to modern physics; Abraham Lincoln, remembered as one of the greatest presidents and leaders of United States; and many others like these we cannot mention. What did all these leaders have in common? What propelled them to turn their initial failures or challenges into eventual successes? None had a direct mentor or inherited any fortune from their parents. Nevertheless, they all eventually succeeded. These people can be distinguished from others based on their self-will to succeed, their self-confidence and belief in themselves, their self-determination, and their perseverance, among other characteristics. The distinguishing characteristics displayed externally in service or relationships toward others are the outward functional attributes that define that leader.

Think about yourself as a student, faculty member, or that new executive. What was it that made your journey to success different and even great? Students and colleagues, when they see or hear about my display of what I have referred to as the 'wilderness walk of faith', have asked me to share the critical attitudinal elements that made me remain inwardly resilient and undaunted and yet outwardly joyful in the difficulties I had faced. This book is the result of those reflections. Let me explain one such teaching moment.

Many years ago, sitting in my research lab on a Saturday morning trying to finish writing my dissertation, a fellow graduate student walked into the room to talk with me. He was contemplating terminating his graduate studies. He was a privileged single male student but felt the load was just too much.

"Sylvanus," he asked, with seriousness in his eyes, "your research advisor suggested that I should ask you, 'what is it that makes you tick?'.'What is it about you that makes you joyful and at peace with yourself and determined to finish, no matter the situations and high expectations we face in this department?"

What he asked me were deeply reflective questions, but I was willing and excited to answer them. Even so, before I do, let's look at the context. At that period in my life, I had four little children as a graduate student; in fact, more children than any of the faculties at that time, except for one faculty member who had eight children. I received little or no support from the department. I was then an international alien, did not qualify for financial aid, and was not given any research assistant position. I was, therefore, self-supported with two off-campus part-time jobs. I joked at being a minority of minorities, the only student in the department with such a label,—but I was self-willed to succeed. My adaptability attribute, coupled with perseverance and resilience, was all that I needed to succeed despite the odds against me. In every exam, homework assignment, or project I had to compete with students with full financial aid, plus they had nothing to distract their attention from their studies. I lived with the attitude that using disadvantages as an excuse was not an option. Aspiring to earn my Ph.D. was a life dream, and I was willing to give my ultimate best to actualize that dream even in the face of challenges. The choice was mine!

So I looked at my classmate and all I could see was a student striding through a valley through which I also walked. He needed me to show him how to walk the walk, to empathize with him. To answer his question, I smiled, not that I wanted to, but because it was just who I was. The joy he attributed to me was an overflow of my appreciation of God's grace that His life in me was externally manifesting His light to bless someone else. It was a great teaching moment; I capitalized on it to tell my classmate that my joy was not about me. He could see physically but about He who was in me, he could not see in the flesh; I needed him to know that I was just showing forth His life in me. At first, my classmate did not understand the spiritual prose or metaphor I was using. He looked surprised but open to hearing more.

I did not ask if he was a Christian. However, right on my desk was my small green pocket Bible. I opened to 2 Corinthians 12:9 (NIV) and handed it to him to read. As he read the passage: "But he said to me, 'My grace is sufficient for you, for my power is made perfect in weakness.' Therefore, I will boast all the more gladly about my weaknesses, so that Christ's power may rest on me," I noticed how absorbed he was in the words

He looked astonished and read it again, this time silently. "This is interesting, but what does this mean?" He asked. I took his question to mean, "How does this relate to my question?

I explained to my friend that the external attitudes he or my advisors saw in me that warranted the question, "What makes you tick" were inspired by my inner value system based on my faith in this same Christ and His teachings. My desire to manifest His life and self-confidence is all because of what He has promised in His word if I believed. I have believed His words and have gained self-determination and faith to make the right choices through Him for my life, and his spirit has given me perseverance and resilience to focus on finishing strong in pursuit of any goal. "With that faith, I have continued, more passionately and excitedly; I can look at my challenges and vulnerabilities and delight joyfully in them, even as an alien minority of minorities! His grace and power have empowered me to do all things I want to do. That is what makes me tick," I explained.

He looked at me as if he got his answer. "Wow, thanks!" he said, looking inspired and ready to face his challenges. As we concluded with a prayer, and he stood up to leave, I pointed empathetically to his face and said, "If I made it despite my challenges, you have absolutely no excuse but to persevere to complete your studies; you can make it too!"

It is fitting to report that this encounter with my classmate transformed his will and determination to continue. Yes, he was encouraged and went on to complete his graduate studies. He emulated self-will and perseverance from the example of the most vulnerable of all students in the department.

The inner value system of a Leader-Servant is founded not only on his faith but his self-will, coupled with self-leadership; it is the greatest mentor who can turn any situation into an inconceivable success. Self-will is the primary driver for determination, resilience, and perseverance. It is what wakes you up in the morning to ask for strength to do whatever it is you are setting out to do. Based on my life walk of faith, I can state with absolute certainty that faith is the unseen assuredness that can empower you to turn your life's probable impossibilities into great and improbable possibilities.

ABOUT LEADER AS SERVANT LEADERSHIP (LSL) MODEL

Looking at the testimony above, do you know the source that energizes the characteristics you display outside and how your inner self is related to what others see outside? What distinguishes you from others is what combines to define your attributes! As a follower, can you identify the characteristics that distinguish your leaders? As an executive, how do you base your evaluation of yourself? Or how do you evaluate that brand-new manager or new youth director you want to hire? To what do you compare the individual's qualities when you look at his CV? What is the basis of your measure? Do you know if you are a substantial leader? These personal questions and much more are the subjects of this two-volume book, 'The Authentic Leader as Servant Part I: The Outward Leadership Attributes, Principles, and Practices', is written in two parts; the second part 'The Leader as Servant Leadership Model. Part II'; deals with the Inner Strength Leadership Attributes, Principles, and Practices.

When we think about today's corporate greed, deepening divide between the haves and have-not, gridlock in political systems, conflicts and wars, high divorce rates, and the rich young ruler in the Bible, it is easy to agree that all these people share a few things in common: self-centeredness, pride, lack of compassion, and greed. There is a great need in today's suffering world for leader-servants who display leadership attributes. These attributes should be oriented toward selfless service to others. Indeed, our world is increasingly drifting away from global serving reality toward the self and apathy. The most credible message or model for a possible solution to this dilemma and the answer to several complex leadership questions can be found in the foundation of the ultimate leader-servant, Jesus Christ. This book defines the Leader as Servant Leadership attribute as the combined acts of two or more distinctive functional leadership characteristics exhibited in service and relationship toward others. There is no better time than now for a book that presents comprehensive and irrevocable facts and principles regarding how to develop effective attributes of the leader-servant.

The Leader as Servant Leadership Model

My first book on this subject, The Leader as Servant Leadership Model, explains that Jesus' servant leadership model is based on the notion of a Leader as a Servant and not on a Servant as Leader. There are four distinct differences between a Servant as Leader (Servant-leader) and the Leader as Servant (leader--servant) models. It is pertinent to highlight them here to connect to this book, Authentic Leader as Servant.

A Leader as Servant is a leader first. The leader–servant as a leader does not in the line of duty go projecting or lording his or her power and authority over others but is the person to lead the process of influencing desired changes in others through his humble example of being a servant or having a serviceable attitude toward others. He or she is a serving leader, not a lording leader. He leads as a servant by putting others' needs above his own needs and rights. Jesus emphasized the word "as" meaning that the leader (the Master) chooses to serve as a servant even though he is the leader. A leader–servant emulates Jesus, who gave up all rights, and emptied and expended Himself on His followers. He empowered them to become more like Him. A leader-servant is known as a leader first but is seen as a great leader by his humble attendant heart and acts of service to others. His greatness comes from his ability to put others above himself.

Leader as Servant is a Biblical Concept. The model or image of a humble serving leader motivated Jesus' disciples to see that if their master could do this for them, they must also be able to do it for others. Jesus clearly demonstrated the process of leader-as-servant leadership. In some cases, He chose to serve by leading when He wanted to create the image or model of the leader-servant in certain acts. In other cases, He chose to lead by serving, when he showed care and empathy toward the people and led the disciples to see empathy as a leadership attribute.

Leader as Servant is an Authentic Leadership Model to follow. The Leader as the Servant leadership model intentionally positions Jesus as an original model of a leader to follow.

He was serving His disciples to demonstrate that the process of becoming a great leader was earned through humble acts of service to others; He made them understand that He was empowering them to succeed Him as leader-servants through service to others. The result was an incomparable legacy of leadership that changed their communities. The fact that Jesus relinquished his rights or shared His power did not diminish His power and influence. In fact, his influence increased at least 11 X 100%, if we ignore the one case of Judas.

The Leader as Servant Transforms Organizational Culture. The proposed LSL model seeks to transform and sustain the community or organization by instilling key leadership values or "leadership presence" among followers or an organization's members. Change is sustained when everyone in the organization takes ownership of the change. Rather than focusing on leading more followers to be great followers who conform to the organizational culture, LSL seeks to lead and empower better leaders to be distinguished leaders and community builders.

There are four distinctions, which clearly differentiate many of the existing servants as Leader-based philosophies in relation to servant leadership from my LSL model. Even in the corporate or institutional worlds, there is nothing better than Jesus on which to base Servant Leadership. There is nothing more authentic and impacting than the servant leadership modeled by the life and teachings of Jesus Christ.

The LSL model uses exploratory questions, scenarios, and graphic visualizations to excite critical thinking in ways no other book on this subject has yet attempted. Several personal testimonies of my wilderness walk of faith with God are used to connect the reader to real-life experiences of the concepts discussed. The riveting effect is that the text engages and encourages the reader to walk through the experiences presented. The aim is to inspire the reader spiritually, mentally, and professionally with this far-reaching exposition on the subject of servant leadership.

ABOUT THE AUTHENTIC LEADER AS SERVANT (ALS)

The *Authentic Leader as Servant* argues that no leadership model is as authentic, other-centered, able to build communities, and productive and service-oriented as the model of our ultimate leader-servant, Jesus Christ. No source can provide a better point of reference than that provided in the Bible. Hence, this book aims to be more than just a text on leadership; it hopes to be a personal discovery for those who aspire to develop effective leadership attributes that grow leaders as servants who ultimately develop thriving other-centered communities. This book presents a comprehensive, biblically-based study regarding how to develop these attributes and how they are applied in a servant leadership process. In this biblical context and for clarity, Servant Leadership means *Leader-as-Servant Leadership*. A *leader-servant* refers to a *leader as a servant*, which is distinct from a servant-leader or servant as leader.

Leader as Servant Leadership attributes are shaped by the Leadership's Inner Value system, which consists of character, motivation, and commitment. The *Authentic Leader as Servant* is presented as a necessary resource to complement my *The Leader as Servant Leadership (LSL) Model*. The LSL model integrates a transformative leadership framework and interactive dimensions of Servant Leadership. Leader as Servant Leadership is a process in which a leader, in his leadership position, purposefully chooses to put others' rights and needs above his positional rights and personal needs. He then serves, enables, and empowers followers for growth that builds a thriving organization. The LSL model looks at the predominant Servant Leadership concepts and shares how they compare with biblical principles on how we should lead and be led.

ABOUT THE ALS COURSES

The three books, *LSL Model* and *The Authentic Leader as Servant (*Parts I and II), together demonstrate that with today's global visions to reach people of all races and cultures, now is the time for an authentic servant's heart of service. Those visions and the leadership processes are most effective with the appropriate leadership attributes centered more on people than on the organization, principles regarding how to develop effective attributes of leader-servant.

The ALS I and II combined presented twenty leaders as servant leadership attributes. The series of ALS courses supply training guide to understand, develop, and practice the attributes in a leadership process. Each course is independent and self-contained and does not depend on completing any other course in the series of 20 courses. It is, however strongly recommended, in fact a must read, that chapters 1 and 2 in each series be covered as they lay the foundation of LSL model on which ALS is based.

ALS (Parts I & II) Course Layout

The *Authentic Leader as Servant (ALS)* leadership (parts I and II) book has been broken down into 20 courses in workbook format to achieve three goals 1) Self-discovery of the acts of developing the attribute under review in the course, 2) deeper understanding of the principles, research and biblical teaching behind the attributes, and 3) Learning the strategies for practicing the attributes.

Instruction

The set of questions following each chapter are designed to serve as a guide to discover, explore, and practice the essential ALS leadership attributes, principles, and practices in leadership process. The questions are comprehensive review based on the content of this specific chapter only.

To maximize the learning outcomes, the learner must read through this chapter and sections. Some referenced scriptures in the book are repeated in the summaries for added review if needed, even though they were discussed in the section in which they apply.

> The exercises that follow each chapter will help you in not only understanding your own strength and weaknesses in your acts of the attribute but will guide you in developing practical strategies you can apply in self-leadership process or helping others grow in leadership
>
> All answers to the questions are contained in the associated chapter or sections; consultation of new sources, except for the reference scriptures, is not needed. Thus, it is expected that you answer the questions after you have read the associated section or chapter of the workbook. The scripture or other references cited are only for references as they already discussed in the book

ALS II Course 1: Adaptability Leadership Attribute—*Flexibility overcomes rigidity in new and changing situations.*

Adaptability is framed as an inner strength quality of a leader in responding to changing needs or situations in a service mission. According to the Army training Handbook, adaptability is "an individual's ability to recognize changes in the environment, identify the critical elements of the new situation, and trigger changes accordingly to meet new requirements." God showed Moses adaptability when he empowered him to use the rod in his hand as an instrument for the mission ahead of him. This course will attempt to give meanings to personal reflective questions to discover the distinguishing characteristics of Leadership Adaptability. Numerous techniques, personal examples, empirical case studies, and applications of the adaptability developing strategies are discussed concepts. Practice questions at the end of each chapter are used to guide your development and to frame meanings out of the content to improve your acts of adaptability in a leadership process.

ALS II Course 2: Courage Leadership Attribute—*Courage is the inner strength of the mind to triumph over paralyzing fears of purposeful action that yields good success*

Courage Leadership Attribute is the lynchpin of effective Servant Leadership that supports the display of all the other attributes? Having the inner strength of character and convictions to persevere and hold on to new and often misunderstood ideas in the face of opposition takes courage—inner strength to triumph over the fear of failure or danger. It is even greater courage to venture into positions or overcome situations that nobody like you, has gone to before or where many better qualified than you had gone and failed. In all cases, they all display courage in the face of obstacles and uncertainties. The success is more about courage than the experience. Can such courage be learned or inspired? How do leaders or successful people in their callings get to their heights of achievements? How can courage be an inner strength within or beyond leadership? How does courage attribute triumph over paralyzing fear? This course explores answers to these questions and more by searching for the distinguishing characteristics of courage. Numerous techniques, personal examples, empirical case studies, including practice questions at the end of each chapter are used to guide your development and to frame meanings out of the content to improve your acts of courage leadership process.

ALS II Course 3: Empathy Leadership Attribute—*A measure of a leader's compassion is the empathic engagement in a follower's experience and state of well-being beyond just expressions of feelings and concerns.*

Empathy attribute is the ability to project one's personality and experiences into another person's thoughts, emotions, direct experience, position, and act toward the wellness of that person. How can a leader walk along with someone in that individual's "wilderness" state of suffering or danger? What motivates a leader to *empathize* with a follower? How is empathy an inner strength leadership attribute? Whether it's in your church, your business, your institution, or in your community, this course provides a comprehensive biblical-based discussion on the role of a leader as a servant in empathizing with those he leads. The aim is to inspire the reader spiritually, mentally, and professionally with this far-reaching exposition on empathy in servant leadership. How can a leader make a lasting positive impact in the lives of those he or she leads? Answers to these and other personal reflective questions are explored in this course on Leadership Empathy Attributes. Numerous techniques, personal examples, empirical case studies, including practice questions at the end of each chapter are used to guide your development and to frame meanings out of the content to improve your acts of empathy leadership process.

ALS II Course 4: Encouragement Leadership Attribute—*The direct measures of encouragement are the inspired strength and quality of uplifted spirit to persevere toward a desired outcome.*

There are times when people want to grow in their potential, want to change their present situation, feel emotionally low in lived experiences, or feel as if they should be appreciated for a job well done. In any of these cases, some encouragement goes a long way to lift up the spirit of someone low. A case study is of the leadership qualities of Barnabas, named the "Son of Encouragement" by the disciples (Acts 4:36), because they saw him as an *encourager*. You can only be an encourager from the strength of your inner personality. The act of encouragement is mostly expressed or *given* to inspire growth or apply a spiritual gift to serve others. What did the disciples see in Barnabas? Obviously, he must have affected them with his acts of encouragement. They saw him as an encourager by his *courage* to *inspire* them at a time they desperately needed to move the ministry forward. This course explores the distinguishing characteristics of encouragement attributes in servant leadership. Each characteristic of encouragement attribute will be discussed in detail with emphasis on strategies of how they can be further developed or practiced by a leader-servant in a leadership process. Practice questions at the end of each chapter are used to guide your development and to frame meanings out of the content to improve your acts of encouragement leadership process.

ALS II Course 5: Initiation Leadership Attribute—*Initiation creates the catalyst for a vision, and the vision when acted upon, produces a desired change.*

The initiation of a process for a desired change is the core of the inner strength of a decisive leader in any leadership process. Initiation leadership is the act of taking step to originate or get something started. In general, initiative is an "individual's action that begins a process, often done without direct managerial influence." The primary outcome of the initiation attribute is that it leads to desired change; something new in the lives of the followers or organization, such as a new growth in followers, a new product or policy in an organization, or a new mission or mission agenda. How do leaders take action to begin a process of change? What are the distinguishing initiation characteristics of leaders such as Moses and Nehemiah in working according to God's agenda? How does a leader conceive a strategic vision for initiation action?. or negotiate his way to influence possible actions toward that vision. This course explores answers to these, and other questions based on examples from Nehemiah (Nehemiah 1:4 through 2:6-8) and Moses and God (Exodus 3 and 4:1-14).

ALS II Course 6: Listening Communication Leadership Attribute
—*Effective communication occurs at the convergence of listening attention, hearing, and understanding of the information transmitted.*

A leader-servant face three important types of communication at one point or the other. At the core is listening ability as the inner strength and ability to receive and understand the meanings of words and messages internally and accurately in a two-way communication process. How does a leader-servant communication with God, the Holy Spirit, and followers (individually or collectively) to be most effective. The course explores how the three elements—words spoken, unspoken, and in the spirit—offer unique reflections of the communication process and what they share in common. How does listening serve as a critical element of effective communication between people forms the bridge by which a leader can be effective?. A leader's capacity to listen to communicate effectively depends on the leader's inner strength to perceive, hear, and understand the information from written, verbal, and non-verbal exchanges. Each characteristic of listening communications attribute will be discussed in detail with emphasis on strategies of how they can be further developed or practiced by a leader-servant. Practice questions at the end of each chapter are used to guide your development and to frame meanings out of the content to improve your acts of listening leadership process.

ALS II Course 7: Navigation Leadership Attribute—*Leaders who prepare for and chart through a purposeful course of action arrive with their followers at the desired destination.*

The navigation attribute is having a *vision* for the intended destination plus the direction to get there. Having a vision is a quality of the inner strength of a leader and the path that the leader follows in the life journey is often influenced by internal and external factors. The organizational culture and climate collectively combine to make an organization unique through the diversity of employees' characteristics, values, needs, attitudes, and expectations. How does a leader-servant *navigate* and *negotiate* his actions through the organization and people he serves, individually or collectively, to *finish* or *arrive* at his purpose? How do you prepare your followers to *finish* strong or *arrive* at their destinations? This course explores answers to these and other questions and how a leader's inner strength capacity can empower him to navigate the cultural bridges to influence the desired change in others in their personal and professional needs and attitudes.

ALS II Course 8: Responsibility Leadership Attribute—*Leadership responsibility is the measure of the quality of a Leader's accountability for the growth of followers and the organization*

Responsibility leadership refers to possessing the capability and accountability needed in the act of being responsible (trustworthy, dependable, honest, etc.) in a leadership process. At a personal level, it defines the level of your position (pastor, deacon, department head, janitor, etc.) in your church, family, or employment. Responsible leaders in their positions *choose* to emphasize the positive, uplifting, and flourishing side of organizational life. Are there qualities in your position that need to be trained or developed to influence positive outcomes in people and organizations? Organizationally, what are the attributes of the leadership structure, process, and culture that are most conducive for maximizing the growth of followers and organizations in service toward others? How can responsibility qualities be developed to enhance high-quality relationships, emotional competencies, positive communication, beneficial energy development, and positive climates for the effective leader as a servant leadership process? The course explores answers to these and other questions. Distinguishing leadership characteristics of responsibility attributes are identified and discussed in detail. Practice questions at the end of each chapter are used to guide your development and to frame meanings out of the content to improve your acts of responsibility leadership process.

ALS II Course 9: Stewardship Leadership Attribute—*A measure of good stewardship is the entrustments' better and richer growth change at the end than at the beginning*

Stewardship leadership is the process of utilizing and managing the resources entrusted to you by someone. We recognize that God has ownership of everything above, and below the earth. In that context, we are all stewards of what God owns, including our lives but entrusted to us to be managed and maintained in a purposeful manner that will honor God. What are the distinctive servant leadership characteristics of stewardship and how can they be developed? This course explores answers to these questions with reference to servant leadership. Practice questions at the end of each chapter are used to guide your development and to frame meanings out of the content to improve your acts of steward leadership process

ALS II Course 10: Vision Leadership Attribute—*You have a vision when you understand how you get to your mission-purpose and what the future outcome will be relative to your present.*

The vision leadership attribute gives the leader the ability to specify in the present *what* each follower's or group's growth should be in the future, *where* to focus these efforts to meet that growth; *how* he will accomplish all aspects of his mission, *which* future (destination) he aspires to lead the people, and *when* the purpose will be achieved. Leadership without direction leads followers to nowhere. Vision is the most common descriptor of effective leadership and must be clear and inspirational in order to achieve desired purpose. What are the qualities a visionary leader? When was the last time you added brand new challenges to your normal routine to achieve a new you? Answers to these and other questions are explored in this course. The primary characteristics of visionary leadership will be identified and used to frame a principle of leadership vision attribute. Practice questions at the end of each chapter are used to guide your development and to frame meanings out of the content to improve your acts of encouragement leadership process.

Referenced Scriptures

A variety of Bible translations from over 11,200 original Hebrew, Aramaic, and Greek words to about 6,000 English words do exist with variations in meanings and emphases. I am not a biblical scholar and do not pretend to be one; Hence, I have avoided researching the roots of these words and personally prefer New King James Version (NKJV). I have intentionally used other translations for three main reasons; first, to allow for increased impact and alignment of words to the most desired meaning and emphasis in the concepts being addressed. Second, I wanted new and personal discovery of meanings from translations with which I have not been familiar. And third, I wanted to allow readers who may desire translations other than the NKJV the benefit of their preferred translations. Hence, in addition to the NKJV, other translations used in the book include New International Version (NIV), New Living Translation (NLT), King James Version (KJV), English Standard Version (ESV), and Good News Translation (GNT). Unless otherwise specified, NKJV should be assumed.

Sylvanus Nwakanma Wosu

CHAPTER 1
UNDERSTANDING LEADERSHIP ATTRIBUTES

Leadership attribute is the combined acts of two or more distinctive functional leadership characteristics exhibited in service and relationship toward others.

The starting point of our discussion is the understanding of the key functional definitions and concepts that describe the theme of this book. In general, 1 will define leadership as an integrative process in which a person applies appropriate attributes to guide and influence the sought-after attitudinal changes in others toward accomplishing a particular goal. Specifically, the Leader as Servant Leadership is a process in which a leader intentionally chooses to put the follower's rights and needs above his positional rights and personal needs, and serves, enables, and empowers them for desired spiritual and professional growth that builds thriving communities.

FUNCTIONAL DEFINITIONS

In the context of these definitions, I will begin the descriptions of the leadership attributes of an authentic leader-servant by offering a functional definition of Leadership Attributes, and showing how that definition differs from those of Leadership Character, Characteristics, and Traits.

Leadership Character is the sum total of personal qualities in leadership, such as honesty, values, vision, trust, and so on that make up the moral capital of the leader; Leadership character should describe who the leader is inside or the leader's basic personality traits.

The Leadership Characteristics describe the distinctive characteristics or features of a leader, such as attitudes, competencies, skills, and specific experiences that go beyond his character (personality). Leadership characteristics determine how (through skills and competencies) the leader leads or take actions in the process of leadership in any particular situation;

The Leadership traits are the distinguishing leadership characteristics of a leader (these are things that define his leadership characteristics), which differentiate from personality traits... Leadership traits are the set of characteristics that define a particular leader's leadership. This means that a leadership characteristic is a trait when it is a unique characteristic of the leader.

Leadership Attributes, unlike leadership character, characteristics, and traits, is *a leadership attribute and the combined act of two or more distinctive functional leadership characteristics exhibited in service and relationship toward others* or traits externally displayed in action toward others. All leadership attributes grow out of the leadership inner value system but can be externally displayed predominantly as an outbound or outward attribute or both:

1. **Outbound Attributes:** These are distinctive outward-bound attributes emanating from the inner strength of the leader to support external conduct in service and relationships toward others. They form the internal core functional qualities that motivate or enhance the outward manifestation of the inside character toward others. The outbound attribute such as listening and vision, for example, are the direct results of the inner values of the leader such as patience, hearing, love, humility, or all the fruits of the spirit.

2. **Outward Attributes:** These are distinctive functional outward outer visible attributes emanating from the richness of the outbound and inner values of the leader. For example, external attributes such as Servanthood, emulation/modeling, empathy, etc. are outflows from the leader who will directly impact the follower. Outward attributes can be enriched by the outbound (inner) attributes. As shown in Figure 1, the outward attributes in general form the outer core of

functional attributes in the leader as servant leadership, but they can share some overlapping functions with the outbound attributes.

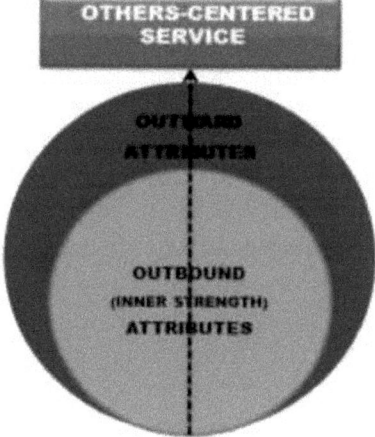

Figure 1.1. Servant leadership functional attributes

In summary, a leadership attribute is more than an ability or a characteristic; it is making those characteristics or abilities functional as part of how the leader acts (his habits) in service to others and applying those characteristics (beyond just having them) in personal and service relations to others. The character or known characteristic defines some aspects of your abilities or who you are inside— e.g. honest, humble, brave, etc. Your attribute, on the other hand, defines your habits; a display of how you use your characteristics, or the actions you exhibit toward others because of who you are inside. For example, empathy as a leadership characteristic becomes a leadership attribute if the followers can distinguish the leader's acts or habits of empathy, such as walking through with his followers in their state of suffering to bring wholeness; otherwise, it is just a characteristic or ability. Leadership attributes toward others are what impact the followers' and the organizational growth more than ability and competence.

In addressing one of the self-righteous hypocritical attributes of servitude leadership, Jesus called leader-servants to be "inside-out" leaders that reflect credibility; indeed, leaders should not appear outwardly righteous when they are full of hypocrisy and lawlessness in their hearts. He was describing "inside–out" as an authentic leadership attribute measured by the display of credibility a leadership attribute!

The measuring stick of a leader-servant is Jesus Christ. We measure ourselves unto the measure of the status of the fullness of Christ (Ephesians 4:13).

The leadership attributes of an authentic leader as a servant are encapsulated in **SERVANT/SERVING LEADERSHIP** are listed in Table 1.1, and defined in Table 1.2: *Servanthood, Emulation, Responsibility, Vision, Navigation, Adaptability, Trust, Listening, Empathy, Affection, Discipleship, Encouragement, Reproduction, Stewardship, Healing-Care, Initiation, Integrity,* and *Persuasion*. Other support attributes include *Influence, Courage, and Generosity*.

The attributes have been separated into Outward and Outbound (Inner Strength) leadership Attributes. As shown in Table 1.1, each of these attributes has three or more leadership characteristics. As such, more than 65 leadership characteristics are covered in these 20 attributes. For example, a leader's Servanthood leadership attribute is characterized by his willing servant's heart of selfless role humility, sacrifice, and submissiveness. The more these are present in a leader, the more effective the servant leadership.

Table 1.1: The functional leader-servant leadership Outbound (Inner Strength) and Outward attributes

	LEADER-SERVANT LEADERSHIP ATTRIBUTES			INNER STRENGTH ATTRIBUTES	OUTWARD ATTRIBUTES
S	Servanthood	L	Listening	Adaptability	Affection
E	Emulation	E	Empathy	Courage	Discipleship
R	Responsibility	A	Affection	Empathy	Emulation
V	Vision	D	Discipleship	Encouragement	Generosity
A	Adaptability	E	Encouragement	Initiation	Healing–Care
N	Navigation	R	Reproduction	Listening	Influence
T	Trust	S	Stewardship	Navigation	Persuasion
I	Influence	H	Healing –Care	Responsibility	Reproduction
G	Generosity	I	Initiation	Stewardship	Servanthood
C	Courage	P	Persuasion	Vision	Trust/Integrity

The list does not assume that a leader has to be excellent in all attributes or even have all of them to be an effective Leader–Servant. However, the more of these attributes the leader displays in his acts of

CHAPTER 1
UNDERSTANDING LEADERSHIP ATTRIBUTES

service toward others, the more productive he or she will be, and the further his impact on the followers and organization. The table also shows that two or more attributes can share common characteristics, which can be applied or observed in different contexts. For example, a leader's ability to inspire followers can be seen in his acts of discipleship, empowerment, an.d encouragement attributes in the context in which these attributes apply. Each attribute is exhibited either as a part of the outbound inner strength attribute of a leader or a part of the outward attribute. Table 1.1 is not an exhaustive list of attributes; in fact, there are hundreds of such attributes. This is just the starting point.

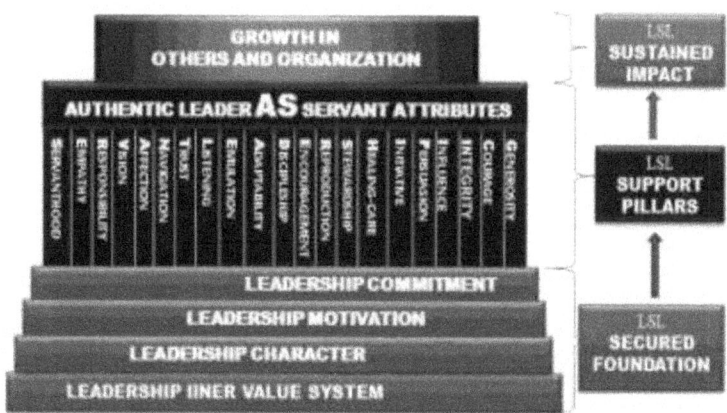

Figure 1.2: Servant leadership outward attributes (dark blue) and relationship to four foundational layers of the LSL Model

Figure 1.2 shows that the leader's attributes are shaped and secured by his four foundational layers (leadership inner value system, leadership character, motivation, and commitment). The attributes of the leader–servants are also conceptualized as the support pillars that will establish and support the personal authenticity of the leader, what the leader, does and the effectiveness of the leadership process. Thus, the attributes represent functional pillars of authentic leadership that can be learned or enriched as described in detail in the subsequent chapters. The combined effect of a secured foundation and stable support pillars will make a sustained impact on the growth of followers and the organization.

COMPARISONS WITH OTHER WORKS

The original works by Greenleaf (1970) in servant leadership [1] have been reviewed by Larry Spears (1996), who identified listening, empathy, healing, awareness, persuasion, conceptualization, foresight, stewardship, commitment to the growth of others, and building community as the ten distinguishing characteristics of servant leadership. [2] Russell (2001) has studied these attributes and have shown them to be essential in servant leadership and concluded that these qualities generally "grow out of the inner values and beliefs of individual leaders." [3] Russell and Stone (2002) extended the Greenleaf 10 attributes to 20 attributes observed in servant-leaders. These 20 attributes were categorized by these authors as either functional attributes (intrinsic characteristics of servant-leaders) or accompanying attributes (complement attributes that enhance the functional attributes).[4] The operational attributes were identified as vision, honesty, integrity, trust, modeling, service, pioneering, appreciation, and empowerment with the accompanying attributes of communication, credibility, competence, stewardship, visibility, influence, persuasion, listening, encouragement, teaching, and delegation. Only three of the attributes identified by Greenleaf were identified, and all three were accompanying attributes rather than functional. Responsibility, adaptability, affection, discipleship, navigation, and reproduction attributes which are considered critical in biblical-based servant leadership in my LSL model are not covered by Russell and Greenleaf. As shown in the description of the attributes in Table 1.2, most of the attributes reported by Russell and Stone (2002)[5] or Greenleaf [1] can be seen either in the twenty attributes or their associated characteristics. Integrity and honesty for example are leadership characteristics of trust and other attributes rather than an independent attributes. I take the position that servant leadership attributes are functional attributes in acts of duty to others and emanate from the inner value system of the leader.

CHAPTER 1
UNDERSTANDING LEADERSHIP ATTRIBUTES

Table 1.2: Description of the functional leader-servant outward leadership attributes and associated principles and characteristics

Leader–Servant Leadership Attributes	Principles of Leadership Attributes	Leadership Characteristics
Affection: *This is the combined love-based works toward providing the essential help or services for the spiritual growth or survival of another person..* (Chapter 2)	*Affection flows from a person to produce positive emotions for the well-being of another person*	Kindness Compassion Practical Love Affective signs Appreciation
Discipleship: *This is the combined acts of personally developing, intentionally equipping, and attentively empowering growth in others to reproduce a heart of service.* (Chapter 3)	*Discipleship transforms and empowers followers for service leadership that grows communities.*	Inspiring Shepherding Equipping Developing Empowering
Emulation: *This is the combined acts of initiating an authentic servant attitude as a model of service worthy of following* (Chapter 4)	*A great leader-servant outwardly and positively inspires a pattern of good works for others to follow.*	Inspiration Motivation Initiation Model Following
Generosity: *This is the combined acts of freely sharing with and giving to others as an act of kindness, without expectation of reward or return to him.* (Chapter 5)	*Generosity is an outward measure of the level of sacrifice, what is shared, or the impact a giving makes, not just the size of the giving.*	Sharing Giving Kindness Affection Love
Healing-Care: *This is the combined acts of providing comfort and empathy to make others whole emotionally and spiritually along with tending to the follower's physical and mental well-being.* (Chapter 6)	*Comforting others in any trouble with the comfort with which we are comforted by God, brings healing - wholeness.*	Self-Healing Empathy Reconciliation Comfort Relational
Influence: *This is the combined acts of positively affecting desired change in conduct,*	*The true measure of leadership success in affecting*	Model Positive attitude Authority

41

performance, and relational connections toward others-centered course of action or service. (Chapter 7)	*desired change in conduct, performance, and relational connections in others is influence*	Connection Wisdom Intelligence,
Persuasion: *This is the combined acts of communicating perspective to connect, challenge, and convince with a compelling purpose to convert others to a new position.* (Chapter 8)	*The means of transforming others to a new perspective is through empathetic persuasion*	Connecting Challenging Communicating Convincing Converting Encouraging
Reproduction: *This is the combined acts of developing your leadership qualities in others and releasing them as successors to continue a greater mission.* (Chapter 9)	*Great leaders produce successors for legacy and greater courses as an expected product of an effective leadership reproduction.*	Selecting Mentoring Equipping Empowering Releasing
Servanthood: *This is the combined acts of humility, willingness, and intentionality in service to others through selfless sacrifice and submission as a servant.* (Chapter 10)	*A leader-servant is most qualified to lead when most ready to serve as a servant for the growth of others. The role of a leader is to serve as a servant*	Servant's heart Humility Sacrifice Service Willingness Submissiveness
Trust*:* *This is the combined acts of positive display of character, competence, credibility, and shared relational connections that produce assured trust-confidence of the trustee in the trusted.* (Chapter 11)	*True leadership trust produces assured trustee's confidence and readiness to follow based on the credibility, competence, and shared relational connections of the trusted.*	Character Competence Integrity Credibility Confidence

PRINCIPLE OF LEADERSHIP ATTRIBUTE

In the context of servant leadership, a leadership attribute is a level above the leadership characteristic or trait of a leader. The principle of leadership attribute states that every leadership attribute has a set of distinguishing characteristics that make up the inward or outward display of the attribute. The principle reflects the essential designed purpose or outcome of the attribute or the inevitable consequence of the effective practice of the attribute. Thus, the principle of leadership attribute is a concise statement about the fundamental truth, value, or belief about the attribute in a leadership situation; it is a statement that establishes an idea about the outcome of the attribute for guiding the practical application of the attribute and its characteristics. I will postulate and frame each principle as an additive function of the characteristics of the attribute. A statement of each principle is quoted at the beginning or below the title of each chapter. It is yet to be experimentally proven if the attribute is a linear or some other non-linear function of these characteristics as variables. It is expected, however, that each character will contribute to the effectiveness of the attribute in varying degrees.

AUTHENTIC LEADERSHIP ATTRIBUTES

At a personal level, attributes are the value-based inside-out moral leadership assets that can be related to the authenticity of a leader-servant. The complexity of defining authenticity has been noted in the literature. The subject of authentic leadership is well covered in the works of Terry (1993),[5] George (2003),[6] and Shair and Eilam (2005).[7] All appear to agree that authenticity requires self-awareness and objective self-identity in personal and social interactions with others. In his book, *Advocacy Leadership*, Professor Gary L. Anderson offers individual, organizational, and societal perspectives on authenticity: "Authenticity, at a peculiar level, is living a life, whether in the private or professional term. This is congruent with one's espoused values; at the structural level, authenticity has to do with viewing human beings as ends in themselves, rather than means to other ends; at the public level, it is a state of affairs that is congruous with the shared political and cultural values of society."[8]

The basic tenets of these perspectives are very fitting to authenticity as a qualifying element of leader-servant leadership attributes. The attribute reflects how the followers see the leader based on the leader's distinctive features displayed through his or her actions personally, organizationally, and societally. The leader is seen as a leader-servant or serving leader because the followers see him lead as a servant from an inside-out value of others. This is what makes the leader authentic.

Authenticity means that what a leader displays outside, in personal or leadership life of service to others, and society is based on the values the leader espouses inside.

Authenticity in servant leadership can be one or two types or both: *Outbound Authenticity and Outward Authenticity*: The Outbound (outward-bound) Authenticity is the genuineness of personal honesty from your inner strength and abilities; what you say and how you act emanate from who you are or how you feel inside. It reflects the essential truth and honesty about your outward-bound inner strength.

Outward authenticity, on the other hand, describes the truthfulness of your credibility and honesty displayed outward in relation to others; your *outer* visible behavior or how you act outwardly towards others reflects exactly your true intentions.

While *outward* authenticity is the visible *outer* indicator of the truth of who you are inside, *outbound* authenticity is outward-bound attribute from the inside of who you are. Credibility in this context is the influence a leader has to attract believability, trustworthiness, and authenticity; it is the believability, trustworthiness, and authenticity of who you are inside and outside.

A key element of personal authenticity is that it is seen or measured in the context of societal, cultural, and organizational interactions. In that context, achieving individual authenticity becomes a challenge since it is influenced by social factors and dispositions of individuals who usually depend on liberal and organizational realities. However, for leader-servant leadership, the leader can face those changing times by remaining focused on his key Biblical-based principles or *Leadership Inner Value System*. Thus, I am interested in authenticity as an essential element of effective Leader-servant leadership attributes or Leader-servant leadership attributes as drivers of leadership authenticity. With that in mind, the first critical element of authenticity in practicing or developing efficient leader-servant leadership attributes is inside-out self-examination relative to the people served rather than the organization. You may ask yourself: What will be my response when the people I lead act or react in a certain way, will it be negative or positive? What are my strengths and vulnerabilities at those times?

Professor Yacobi in his post, "Elements of Human Authenticity," noted that since "the self -arise attribute emerges from interactions between self, others, and the environment in a complex society and

CHAPTER 1
UNDERSTANDING LEADERSHIP ATTRIBUTES

world, there may co-exist multiple complicated identities depending on place and context." [9] He went on to identify the following <u>essential elements of personal authenticity</u>: self-awareness, unbiased self-examination, accurate self-knowledge, reflective judgment, personal responsibility, and integrity, genuineness, and humility, empathy for others, understanding of others, optimal utilization of feedback from others. All of these are covered under the leadership attributes or characteristics shown in Table 1.2.

Bill George, in his book, *Authentic Leadership*, takes the position that to be an authentic leader; a person must have the following essential characteristics: [10]

- Behavior based on value: He must understand his own values and exhibit behavior to others based on those values;
- He must not compromise his values in difficult situations but could use the situation to strengthen personal values in those situations.
- Passion from a clear purpose: Be self-aware of who he is, where he is going, and the right thing to do.
- Compassion from the heart: He must lead from a compassionate heart that allows them to be sensitive to the plight and needs of others,
- Connectedness from a relationship; he must be relationally connected with people he leads,
- Consistency from the self-disciple: He must demonstrate self-discipline to remain calm, collected, and consistent in a stressful situation.

Modeled after the elements above, Table 1.3 lists six essential characteristics of authenticity for servant leadership. These fundamental characteristics cover the five identified above and can also be aligned with the leadership characteristics in Table 1.2. Each attribute in Table 1.2 is expected to pass the personal authenticity test in Tables 1.3, 1.4. In a survey of 132 Christian leaders, seventy-four percent (74%) of them agreed that they always or frequently exhibit servant leadership attributes. [11] Thus, a pass of the outward authenticity test means that a pure leader must demonstrate 70% or more of these essential elements of this legitimacy. (That is, 70% YES in the assessment questions in Tables 1.3, 1.4).

It needs to be noted, however, that a secular leader could be authentic and still lack some of the essential servant leadership attributes or characteristics such as selflessness, servanthood, and love-motivated servant attitudes of a leader-servant. Effective leader-servants are authentic leaders and personal authenticity is an essential element of leader-servant leadership. The key test for leader-servant authenticity is the quality of his inside-out value and personal character. What is most important is a change from the inside-out.

Table 1.3: The test of essential elements of personal inner strength authenticity in servant leadership

	Elements of Inner Strength Authenticity	Inner Strength (Outbound) Authenticity Assessment Questions	YES / NO
1	Personal inside-out value-based behavior	Are your personal inside-out values aligned with acts of service and behavior outside?	1
		Are you honest to yourself in relation to your inner strengths and abilities?	2
2	Inside-out Self-Awareness	Do you have unbiased self-examination, and accurate self-knowledge of who you are inside-out?	3
		Do you know your inner strength and weaknesses in relation to the good you want to show as an outward attribute?	4
3	Inside-out Empathy-Compassion	Do you know and feel from your inside what you want for your followers?	5
		Are you motivated to empathize, based on your inside feelings?	6
4	Inside-out Connection with followers	Do you feel deep, personal, and spiritual connection with your followers?	7
		Does what you say and how you act reflect how you feel when you relate to others?	8
5	Inside-out Emotional Self-regulation	Do you have difficulty controlling your emotion in order to remain calm in a stressful situation?	9
		Are you always able to comfort yourself?	10
6	Inside-out Authenticity Feedback	Do your followers see your inside-out value from your outside behavior?	11
		Will your followers feel that what you say you are is congruent with how you act?	12
#YESs_____; # NOs_____: Outbound Authenticity: YES/ 12-----%			

CHAPTER 1
UNDERSTANDING LEADERSHIP ATTRIBUTES

	Table 1.4: The test of essential elements of personal outward authenticity in servant leadership			
	Elements of Personal Outward Authenticity	Personal Outward Authenticity Assessment Questions	YES or NO
1	Personal value-based outward behavior	Are your personal values and beliefs aligned with your acts of service and behavior toward others?	1
		Do you live out your life according to your beliefs?	2
2	Personal Self-Awareness	Do you have clarity of your personal vision and purpose?	3
		Does what you know about yourself accurately describe what others say?	4
3	Personal Outward Empathy-Compassion	Do you apply how you feel to what your followers need?	5
		Do you lead from a compassionate heart and are you sensitive to the plight and needs of others?	6
4	Personal Connection with followers	Do you feel deep, personal connection with your followers?	7
		Does your outward action toward others reflect exactly your true intentions?	8
5	Outward Emotional Self-regulation	Do you have difficulty controlling your emotions to remain calm in a stressful situation?	9
		Does your evaluation of your value of others agree with how valued they feel?	10
6	Personal Authenticity Feedback	Do your followers see your outward acts as true and honest?	11
		Can your followers see other-centeredness in 70% or more of your attributes?	12
#YESs_____; # NOs_____: Outbound Authenticity: YES/ 12-----%			

ALS COURAGE LEADERSHIP
ATTRIBUTES, PRINCIPLES, & PRACTICES

SUMMARY 1
UNDERSTANDING LEADERSHIP PROCESS

Before starting this exercise, please read and follow the instruction in the preface of this workbook. Answers to these questions are contained in this chapter. Completion of these exercises after reading the chapter should take 60-90 minutes.

Discovering the Leadership Attributes

1. What is your alternative definition of leadership? In learning to lead, how would you differentiate the following elements:
   a. Leadership.
   b. Leader as servant leadership.
   c. Leadership characteristics.
   d. Leadership attributes.
2. What are the key differences between the Leader as Servant and the Servant as Leader Leadership philosophies?
3. What was the original source of the Servant as Leader (SL)? What was the original source of Leader as Servant (LS)?
4. What is the key framework of a Leader as a Servant Leadership?
5. Authenticity in servant leadership can be one or two types or both *Outbound Authenticity and Outward Authenticity*: Describe a time when you displayed:
   a. The Outbound (outward-bound)— *outbound* authenticity is outward-bound attribute from the inside of who you are.
   b. *The Outward Authenticity*—*outward* authenticity is the visible *outer* indicator of the truth of who you are inside,
6. Describe the key elements of personal authenticity seen or measured in the context of societal, cultural, and organizational interactions.
7. How are the essential characteristics of authentic leader in leadership process in challenging times.
8. How much of a leader-servant are you? Take the personal leader-servant audit in Table 1.5 to self-assess your effectiveness.
9. Based on the questions in Table 1.5, can you identify each of the twenty attributes? What ones did you score 3 ("sometimes") or less than 3? Review and learn and commit to work to improve.

CHAPTER 1
UNDERSTANDING LEADERSHIP ATTRIBUTES

Table 1.5. Leader As Servant-Leadership Audit						
A servant-leader in his leadership position purposefully choses to serve and inspire acts of service in others by his example. Select and circle best answer to questions 1=Never: 2=Almost never ; 3=Sometimes; 4=Frequently; 5 =Always						
	Servant Leadership assessment questions	Circle no				
1	I am willing and other-centered, and readily chose to serve others as a servant for their personal growth	1	2	3	4	5
2	I model others-centered attitude in my service and relationships and inspire same for others to follow	1	2	3	4	5
3	I have a sense of obligation, willingness, and accountability for the service towards others	1	2	3	4	5
4	I have the foresightedness to specify in the present view what others' growth should be in a given future	1	2	3	4	5
5	I work toward providing the essential help or services for the spiritual growth or survival of the others;	1	2	3	4	5
6	I provide the needed purposeful course of action for how to chart the course to for my followers.	1	2	3	4	5
7	I display external credibility and a strong sense of character based on values, beliefs, and competence;	1	2	3	4	5
8	In communication, I attentively perceive and hear what is communicated, reflectively listen to understand and to be understood	1	2	3	4	5
9	I walk through with others in their state (suffering, emotions, etc.) in a way that provides the needed care and well-being	1	2	3	4	5
10	I have a measure of self-secured flexibility to adapt appropriate attitude to serve all people in different situations	1	2	3	4	5
11	I personally develop, intentionally equip, and attentively nurture spiritually growth in others	1	2	3	4	5
12	My act of bravery instills in others the courage and confidence to follow or persevere in a course of action	1	2	3	4	5
13	I develop my leadership qualities in others as successors to continue in a purposeful mission	1	2	3	4	5
14	I manage , maintain,, and account for all resources entrusted to me and being responsible for the difference my acts make	1	2	3	4	5
15	As a care-giver, I act to comfort and make others whole emotionally	1	2	3	4	5
16	When I see a need, I originate a vision and action, and stay committed to meet that need and desired change	1	2	3	4	5

ALS COURAGE LEADERSHIP
ATTRIBUTES, PRINCIPLES, & PRACTICES

17	I display a holistic view of an issue to inform, transform or convert others to my view through empathetic persuasion	1	2	3	4	5
18	I freely share what I have sacrificially as an act of kindness to others, without expectation of reward in return	1	2	3	4	5
19	My act of influence is to affect the actions, behavior, opinions, etc., of others based on trust, credibility and relationship	1	2	3	4	5
20	In the face challenges and danger, I act with bravery to overcome fear and take a stand with strength and conviction	1	2	3	4	5
Score Range	Add up the numbers in each column (Total Score____ Check and Understand the key areas to work on					
81-100	Strong Leader-Servant; keep it up, go and train others.					
66-80	Above average Leader-Servant; work 25% of key areas					
50-65	Average but developing; need to work on 50% of key areas					
34-49	Below average leader; work on 75% of key areas					
<34	Not a Leader-Servant; need training in all areas					

CHAPTER 2
COURAGE LEADERSHIP ATTRIBUTE

Courage is the inner strength of the mind to triumph over paralyzing fears of purposeful action that yields good success

Leadership Courage Attribute is intentionally one of the longest chapters for one primary reason: Leader as a Servant Leadership courage attribute is the lynchpin of effective Servant Leadership without which none of the other attributes could be displayed. It requires a much more detailed treatment than most other chapters. All leader-servants need courage as a gut feeling that comes from the inside. Servant Leadership is a transformative fresh kind of leadership model and needs yielded leaders who will not waver in their convictions. Having the inner strength of character and convictions to persevere and hold on to new and often misunderstood ideas in the face of opposition takes courage. It takes courage to adapt to servant leadership philosophies without fear of being considered a weak leader for extending rights to your followers or employee.

Early in my freshman year, I wondered how students before me made it through education up to the Ph.D. level. I even saw people with two or more Ph.Ds. For my graduate studies, I had the courage to persevere to the finish. As a leader, I have also seen and interacted with very highly-placed leaders. In each case, I have come to admire these leaders and usually have one question: how did they get there? It took a lot of courage for anybody to want to run for the office of the president of the United States or the chancellor of a major University, or the CEO of a large corporation. It is even greater courage to venture into positions that nobody like you, has gone to before or where many better qualified than you had gone and failed; such is the case of President Obama. Human history is filled with leaders who have made it to the top from presidents of countries to CEOs of great corporations. In all cases, they all had one thing to come: courage in the face of obstacles and uncertainties. Why do you think such people succeeded? It is more about pure courage rather than the "I have the experience" feeling! These leaders risk public scrutiny and are willing to go through so much to get to the top. So I ask you; what would you consider to be a distinctive driver for courage? Can courage be learned or inspired? How can courage be an inner strength within or beyond leadership? This chapter will explore answers to these questions by searching for the distinguishing characteristics of courage. Based on those characteristics, we can posit definitions of the principle and attribute of leadership courage.

SERVANT LEADERSHIP COURAGE ATTRIBUTE

The acts of courage are displayed in many forms, within and beyond leadership: in peaceful resistance against an oppressor in any situation, tough choices and decisions at work, staying fervent on your convictions, suffering pain for a cause you feel greater than you, risking what is of value to you, in the face of impending danger, and others. These situations present risks of different kinds and different senses of fear of loss of life or freedom. There are so many people in history that displaced courage in the presence of the situations above. Here are just a few of such people in my estimation, who displayed remarkable courage in causes in which they fervently believed:

Rosa Parks and Civil Rights: In the civil rights era in the USA, buses and busing and some public amenities were segregated by race. When Rosa Parks, a black pEolitical activist and secretary of her local chapter of the NAACP, refused to give up her seat at the front of a segregated bus, and risk arrest and violence for her *conviction* of what was right, that was an act of courage outside leadership. [12]

Nelson Mandela's fight against apartheid: South African Blacks, under the policy of Apartheid that from 1948 to 1994 curtailed the rights of the majority of black inhabitants, suffered one of the worst injustices in modern times. Nelson Mandela, who was one of the leaders in the South African resistance to racial segregation, was arrested for treason in 1963 and sentenced to life imprisonment. Nelson Mandela *triumphed* over fears of being killed. Despite spending nearly 27 years in jail, went on to be the first black president in South Africa's history, and led a movement of forgiveness and reconciliation till his death. Those were acts of courage within and beyond leadership. It was this experience that framed his famous quote: "courage is not the absence of fear, but the triumph over it. The *brave* man is not he who does not feel fear, but he who conquers that fear." [13]

Galileo Galilei's science before faith:[14] As a scientist, I like to include one of my heroes in this list. Galileo Galilei was an Italian scientist and devout Catholic. His early scientific discoveries provided evidence for the idea that the earth moves around the sun, which was then considered heretical. When he *risked* ex-communication from the church and accepted imprisonment rather than denying his views, that was an act of courage.

President Barrack Obama gave orders to find and kill Osama: this was during his running for and winning the presidency of the United States. His order and Seal for Team Six to raid and kill Osama bin Laden, the leader of al-Qaeda that master-minded the 9/11 incident that took over 3000 lives, was an act of courage within leadership. In making that decision, the president took on a lot of *risks*—American lives, and a diplomatic or military conflict with Pakistan. He knew that failure in the mission to kill bin Laden could have resulted in an international propaganda victory for al-Qaeda and risk his presidency. Vice President Biden was quoted as saying, "Obama's real act of *valor* was ordering the operation despite the catastrophic possibility that a failed mission, it could have tarnished his reelection chances…Had he failed in that *audacious* mission; he would have been a one-term president." [15] This has been referred to even by his critics as a *decisive* moment for his presidency; a display of *courage* and *risk* by the president.

What does the Bible teach about courage in leadership? The Bible documents leaders, such as David, Samson, and Joshua in Old

Testament, and in the New Testament, Jesus, John the Baptist, Peter, and Paul, who demonstrated courageous leadership.

Joshua showed courageous leadership. Early in Joshua's call to leadership after the death of Moses, the servant of God, God commissioned Joshua to take over in leading the Jews to the Promised Land. The Bible shows that God considered courage as an important attribute of effective leadership. In four verses (Joshua 1:6-9, NIV), God used the words " courage"- or related words- four times, and indicated some key elements of courageous leadership:

> *Be strong and of good courage, for to this people you shall divide as an inheritance... Only be strong and very courageous, that you may observe to do according to all the law... do not turn from it to the right hand or to the left, that you may prosper wherever you go...For then you will make your way prosperous, and then you will have good success. Have I not commanded you? Be strong and of good courage; do not be afraid, nor be dismayed, for the* LORD *your God is with you wherever you go (Joshua 1:6-9, NKJV).*

The promise to Joshua is true for every leader today. You need to be *strong, courageous,* and *careful to obey* and be led by God's ways. And when you have done so, you must not be afraid or discouraged because God will guide you to make your destined journey prosperous and to have good success.

Young David's triumph over Giant Goliath: When David was about 17 years old, and before he became King, Israel had been under terrifying threats of fear from Goliath, a 6 cubits and a span (Approximately 9-11 feet)[1] tall Philistine giant (1 Samuel 17:7), wearing an armor of 125-200 pounds (by best estimate). The Bible records that Goliath, for 40 days (morning and evening) had issued a challenge to Israel to come out to fight him: "I defy the armies of Israel this day; give me a man that we may fight together. When Saul and all Israel heard these words of the Philistine, they were dismayed and greatly afraid" (1 Samuel 17:10-11, NKJV). It was an audacious act of courage when David, the youngest son of Jesse, with no human fighting experience or handling any weapon, even too young to wear protective gear, willingly and

---

[1] Hebrew Bible, 1 cubit =17-22 inches; 1 span = 9 inches

CHAPTER 2
COURAGE LEADERSHIP ATTRIBUTES

bravely requested King Saul to fight this terrorizing giant of Goliath. Saul pointed out to David the physical contrast between him and Goliath, and said to David, "You are not able to go against this Philistine to fight with him; for you *are* a youth, and he a man of war from his youth" (1 Samuel 17:33, NKJV). However, David's *bravery* was his inner strength; this bravery motivated by his understanding of God's strength and power to deliver; he had acquired this convictions from his previous victory over the paws of the lion and the bear. He told King Saul very *decisively*, for this "Uncircumcised Philistine ...the LORD, who delivered me from the paw of the lion and from the paw of the bear, He will deliver me from the hand of this Philistine" (Samuel 17:36-37, NKJV). To Goliath, David *fearlessly* issued his own challenge and threat: "I come to you in the name of the LORD of hosts, the God of the armies of Israel, whom you have defied. This day the LORD will deliver you into my hand, and I will strike you and take your head from you" (I Samuel 17:45-46, NKJV). What audacity! There is no agreement of how tall David was when he fought Goliath. Even still, any height less than 7 feet and being young; standing in comparison to this man who was close to an 11 feet huge giant (with all fighting gear and spear of intimidating size and length) and issuing threats as David did, would look like a joke. David's brothers, King Saul and the army of Israel from a human perspective did not think he could defeat this giant either. Yet, David looked at Goliath and was *self-willed* to issue his own threat in the face of tremendous human odds against him. David was disgusted by the sight and voice of this uncircumcised Philistine defying the army of God of Israel. When courageous leaders are disgusted with a desperate situation, they fearlessly act in revolt against the situation. Thus, his courage was also driven by his conviction and outright rejection of the paralyzed state of the army of Israel in front of the danger with no one with the courage to lead. David triumphed over Goliath not because of his own outward size or strength, but because of his inner-strength courage based on his trust and confidence in the Lord. He never wavered in his *convictions* and gave God the glory for the victory.

John the Baptist's boldness with his message of repentance: (Matthew 3:1-10) John the Baptist demonstrated courageous leadership as the fore runner of Jesus in several ways: He called people to repentance, confronting and pointing out their hypocrisy. He displayed boldness:

his message was *direct* and purposeful; he was *decisive* in the delivery and content of the message. Without the fear of his own life, imagine a young leader like John demonstrating blunt *bravery* and *conviction* in his vision and method. For example, he called the most powerful people of influence in his time (the Pharisee and Sadducees), "You brood of vipers! Who warned you to flee from the coming wrath? Produce fruit in keeping with repentance" (Matthew 3:7-8, NIV).

The Apostles and the work of the Gospel— Peter, Paul, and John all displayed courageous leadership in carrying forward the Gospel even at the threats of their lives. Peter exuded common characteristics of courage in leadership when he and John, were thrown into jail for preaching that salvation is only through Jesus and for performing miracles in the name of Jesus (Acts 4: 10-13). Nevertheless, when their captors asked by whose authority the man was healed, Peter displayed *no fear* but was *bold to* proclaim that it was through the name of Jesus; his message about how they crucified Jesus was very direct, purposeful, and audacious. The Bible confirms that "When they saw the courage of Peter and John and realized they were unschooled, ordinary men, they were astonished, and they took note that these men had been with Jesus" (Acts 4:13, NIV).

The same tenets for courage were also demonstrated by Apostle Paul in reproducing himself in Timothy and preparing this young man for leadership. Paul taught Timothy, and all other prospective leaders that courage is the act of taking a stand in difficult, often challenging situations, such as courage to flee from evil youthful desires, courage to pursue righteousness, faith, love, and peace, courage not to have anything to do with foolish and stupid arguments, courage not to be quarrelsome but to be kind to everyone, able to teach and to not be resentful (2 Timothy 2:22-26). John Maxwell in *The Maxwell Leadership Bible* noted that "Courage is the first essential quality of leadership. Leaders initiate and take a stand when no one else travels with them." [15]

PRINCIPLE OF LEADERSHIP COURAGE ATTRIBUTE

The above examples and scriptures reveal that the primary characteristics of being courageous are to be *strong, brave (bold, audacious), self-willed, and fearless* in their *convictions*. Furthermore, to be courageous calls for *full faith* and regular submission to God by making the Principle of God one's daily guide. The leader must meditate and remain under God's command. A courageous leader must also encourage himself with the promise and presence of God, and he must have the mindset that God is his all-sufficiency and source of strength; he must be very bold and *decisive,* but he must also be careful to serve by leading only according to the word of God. His courage and hope of success in his calling and the challenges ahead depend on full and consistent adherence to the Principle of God. Based on these characteristics, we posit the following:

The Servant Leadership Courage –Attribute is combined acts of overcoming fear and taking a stand with strength, conviction, bravery, self-will, and decisiveness in full submission to God.

The primary purpose of courage in leadership is to lead by taking a stand in a situation. The strength as a tool to be courageous is based on your leadership inner value system and the Word of God, walking with God and being careful to obey and lead by it. Your spiritual strength empowers the self-will and self-determination that culminate in a decision to take a stand. Each of these four stages is critical in effectively displaying the courageous leadership attribute. The expected outcomes or rewards of a courageous leadership attribute that submits to God are a good success, prosperity, and fruitful leadership. Good success, by my earlier definition, is the achievement of something that is of eternal value to God. This can be stated as follows;

The Servant Leadership Courage principle is Courage in the inner strength of the mind to triumph over the paralyzing fear of purposeful actions that will yield good success

The principle of servant leadership courage –attribute is modeled in Figure 3 and expressed as:

BRAVERY + STRENGTH + SELF-WILL + DECISIVENESS = COURAGE

Figure 3: Servant leadership courage-attribute model

Figure 3 shows that courage is initiated by the bravery to face your challenges and overcome the paralyzing fear to take action based on your inner strength of character that drives yourself-will and decisiveness.

LEARNING TO BE COURAGEOUS

The examples of leaders above are just a few of the several leaders in the Bible that showed great courage in leadership. What about you? Or some leaders you know? Are you being courageous in your walk with God? In learning to be courageous, what would you say is missing that you want to work on—strength, bravery, self-will, or decisiveness? Is fear paralyzing your courageous leadership? See how you can improve in any of these characteristics of courageous leadership attributes:

Courage Bravery: The courage and audaciousness of overcoming the fear that paralyzes your courageous leadership or ability to take purposeful action; being open to direction and change.

Courage Strength: The spiritual strength needed to build courage or initiate courageous action— taking the first stand in pursuing bold and new ideas, building confidence in yourself and others.

Courage Self-Will: Courage of self-leadership and self-determination of building confidence in yourself and others; self-regulation of your emotions and exercise of faith in people.

CHAPTER 2
COURAGE LEADERSHIP ATTRIBUTES

Courage Decisiveness: The courage of readily making tough decisions in face of challenging issues, comfortable criticism, and opinions; the absence of equivocation to take purposeful action

SUMMARY 2
COURAGE LEADERSHIP ATTRIBUTE

Before starting this exercise, please read and follow the instruction in the preface of this workbook. Answers to these questions are contained in this chapter. Completion of these exercises after reading the chapter should take 60-90 minutes.

Discovering Courage Leadership Attribute

1. What is Courage leadership Attribute and why is it the lynchpin of effective Servant Leadership?
2. What would you consider to be a distinctive driver for courage?
3. How can courage be an inner strength within or beyond leadership? How can the acts of courage be displayed?
4. What are the distinguishing characteristics of courage leadership? Which of the these applies most to you?
5. What does the Bible teach about courage in leadership in leaders like David, Samson, and Joshua in Old Testament, and in the New Testament, Jesus, John the Baptist, Peter, and Paul,.
6. How did God consider courage as an important attribute of effective leadership (Joshua 1:6-9, NIV),
7. When courageous leaders are disgusted with a desperate situation, they fearlessly act in revolt against the situation (1 Samuel 17:10-46, NKJV). What drove David's courage in those situations, where did that come from and what was the outcome?
8. How did John the Baptist demonstrate courageous leadership as the fore runner of Jesus (Matthew 3:1-10)
9. How did The Apostles and the work of the Gospel display courageous leadership in carrying forward the Gospel (Acts 4:13, NIV; (2 Timothy 2:22-26).

Understanding the Principle of Courage Leadership Attribute

1. What are primary characteristics of being courageous
2. As a principle what does being courageous called for in a leader?
3. The primary purpose of courage in leadership is to lead by taking a stand in a situation. State the *Servant Leadership Courage principle*
4. State the additive law of courage leadership attribute

Practicing Courage Leadership Attribute

1. What meaning or lesson can you frame the experience of reading this chapter?
2. List the four characteristics of courage leadership attributes you have
3. List five Traits of courageous leaders
4. What are the common sources of fear and give 3-5 Strategies for Overcoming Fear?
5. How many acts of courage as an attribute do you display? Take the leadership courage attribute audit in Table 2.1. See how you can improve in any of these characteristics of courageous leadership attributes:
   a. **Courage Bravery**
   b. **Courage Strength**
   c. **Courage Self-Will.**
   d. **Courage Decisiveness**

Table AII.2. Leadership Courage Attribute Audit

The Servant Leadership Courage –Attribute is combined acts of overcoming fear and taking stand with strength, conviction, bravery, self-will, and decisiveness in full submission to God. Assess the quality of your acts of courage by inserting an X below the number that best describes your response to each statement.

Item	Acts of Courage Attribute Check 1= Always; 2= Frequently; 3= Sometimes; 4= Almost Never; 5= Never	1	2	3	4	5
1	I have inner strength to overcome the paralyzing effects of fear					
2	I have the spiritual strength needed to take first stand in pursuing new ideas,					
3	Others see bravery and inner strength in me in the face of challenges					
4	I keep the lines of communication open and not afraid to share information instead of hoarding it.					
5	My courage in my acts of influence on others is purposefully driven toward service					
6	I am able move forward with decisions without the crutch of 'analysis paralysis'					
7	I am self-secured and willingly give credit to those around me					
8	I hold people (and myself) accountable for appropriate behaviors					
9	I take purposeful action with bravery in the direction for change.					
10	I am not afraid of confronting people's issues or taking appropriate action on performance					
	Add up your rating in each column					
Score Range	Guide and Explanation of Score: understand the areas to develop	Total Score=				
10-17	Great courageous leader; keep it up!					
18-25	Above Average- courageous leader; need to work on (25%) of the areas					
26-33	Average courageous leader; need to work on (50%) of the areas					
34-41	Below average courageous leader ;need to work on (75%) of the areas					
42-50	Not a courageous leader ; need to work on all the key areas					

CHAPTER 3
DEVELOPING COURAGE–BRAVERY

Courage-bravery is the courage and audacity of overcoming the fear that paralyzes your courageous leadership. In the words of Nelson Mandela, "The brave man is not he who does not feel fear, but he who conquers that fear." [13] So bravery is a leader himself or herself overcoming fear in any situation. It is the first critical act of courage. Fear the Devil's primary weapon of war against a Leader-Servant. Peter's vulnerability, while he walked on water toward Jesus was fear. The Bible says that "God has not given us a spirit of fear but of power (of Bravery and strength) and of love and a sound mind" (II Timothy 1:7). We frequently face fears, including the natural, innate fears that help us respond to impending danger in the flight or fight attitude. Fear has a paralyzing and controlling impact on a leader's faith as has many sources.

A 2011/2012 report by a multi-disciplinary team of expert psychologists and researchers in IBM [16] showed that workplace stress is driven in most part by fear in which people- rank and file and management- tend to avoid taking a tough stand on issues to survive. The report was based on a survey of over 31,000 workers from 28 countries about workplace issues such as managerial and leadership effectiveness, senior management behavior, diversity practices, turnover intentions, and job satisfaction. In addition to impending danger as a source of fear, other sources of fear include:

1. Perceived threats precipitated from horror and terror.
2. Uncertainties.
3. Warfare and battles in wars.
4. Tragedies or disasters.
5. Threatening situations of impending danger.
6. Illness or sicknesses.
7. Working into unknown situations.
8. Past experiences, failures, relationships.

9. Unwillingness to give up power and control is seen in many dictatorial leaders.
10. Negative attitudes develop into low self-esteem, low self-confidence, or low self-image.
11. Lack of a close walk, faith, trust, confidence, and understanding of security in God.
12. Weak sense of character and purpose

Develop strategies for overcoming fear

The subject of overcoming the paralyzing effects of fear, and biblical promises as part of the weapons and tools a leader can use to overcome the challenges of fear, are fully discussed in my book, *The Leader as Servant Leadership Model.* [10.] Principle #9 of Walking with God for Good Works states that "Walking with God gives us the courage to overcome fear." [10] Bravery for overcoming fear comes from depending on God's promises and acting in obedience to the associated responsibility as God instructed Joshua to do. Developing bravery in courage as an attitude starts by developing personal strategies to overcome fear. Some of the examples are summarized below*:*

Trust God as your tower of safety. "The LORD is my rock, my fortress, and my deliverer; my God is my rock, in whom I take refuge, my shield and the horn of my salvation, my stronghold; The name of the LORD is a fortified tower; the righteous run to it and are safe (Psalm 18:2,10 NIV). This was part of the song David sang to the Lord when He delivered him from his enemies. Our trust must be in God alone who will save us from any impending danger.

As junior faculty many years ago, I was called to chair a department with absolutely no prior leadership experience. However, the Dean called me in and laid this role on me, with no second choice to fill the position. My first emotion was fear. I was afraid of failure, of disappointing him, mainly because of impending challenges I perceived from professors who were much more senior than I was, and who I had seen tore down the previous chairperson. I was encouraged by the fact that King David looked at God as his rock to run to. If leaders build their work on Jesus as the rock, they will not have to fear. Jesus advised that we must have our foundation in Him as the rock "The rain came down, the streams rose, and the winds blew

CHAPTER 3
DEVELOPING COURAGE–BRAVERY

and beat against that house; yet it did not fall, because it had its foundation on the rock." Jesus is the rock (Matthew 7:25).

Increase the presence of the Lord to cast away fear. This is the secret of courageous leadership that yields good success as God himself advised Joshua. Jesus calls us to come and be yoked with him with those things that weigh us down and cause us to fear. "Come to me, all you who are weary and burdened, and I will give you rest" (Matthew 11:28 NIV). Spending time with the Lord—in His Word, praying, and listening to the Lord, is the surest way to build the kind of trust that dispels fear. His presence presents safety and joy. When Jesus stepped into the boat with Peter, His presence stilled the storm and dispelled their fears. David said, "Whoever dwells in the shelter of the Most High will rest in the shadow of the Almighty. Surely, he will save you from the fowler's snare and from the deadly pestilence. He will cover you with his feathers" (Psalm 91:1-5). The result of living under the presence of God is the assurance of His protection over us.

Take safety and bravery in the promises of God. All the sources of fear listed thus far and more can be overcome through faith and living based on God's promises. God reminds us in His Word that we are not only to depend on his promises but to constantly and persistently remind ourselves of the promises when we pray when we are faced with difficulties. He said, "You (leaders) who make mention (pray) of the Lord, do not keep silent (to remind Him of His promises). And give Him no rest till He establishes, And till He makes Jerusalem a praise in the earth" (Isaiah 62:6–7 NKJV). Faith is the building block of a leader's inner strength.

God gave His servants, from Adam to Jesus, precious promises from which they could find safety. The Apostle Peter described it this way: "Whereby are given unto us exceedingly great and precious promises: that by these ye might be partakers of the divine nature, having escaped the corruption that is in the world through lust," (2 Peter 1:4). The promises equip leaders with support from God to escape challenges in this corrupt world. Peter reminded Christians and church leaders of this when he said, "His divine power has given us everything we need for a godly life through our knowledge of Him who called us by His own glory and goodness. Through these, he has given us His very great and precious promises, so that through them, you may participate in the divine nature, having escaped the corruption in the world caused by evil desires" (2 Peter 1:3-4).

INNER STRENGTH PROMISES TO OVERCOME FEAR

Here are a few promises to remember when you are faced with these common sources of fear [10]

1. **Fear when you are weak.** You, like Paul, can do all things through Christ, who strengthens you: "I can do all things through Christ who strengthens me" (Philippians 4:13, NKJV). *Understand that God is with you with His own strong Hand: "thou art with me; thy rod and thy staff they comfort me (Psalm 23:4);* Understand that God is your light and source of your strength: "The LORD is my light and my salvation; whom shall I fear? The LORD is the strength *of my life; of whom shall I be afraid?" (Psalm 27:1, KJV)*

2. **Fear when faced with the enemy attack.** *No* weapon that Satan can fashion against you shall prosper; for this is the will of God. God declared, "No weapon forged against you will prevail, and you will refute every tongue that accuses you" (Isaiah 54: 15–17, NIV). He that is with God is a mighty army.

3. **Fear from challenges from all side**s. Remember the words of Paul, "We are hard pressed on every side, but not crushed; perplexed, but not in despair; persecuted, but not abandoned; struck down, but not destroyed" (Philippians 4:8–9, KJV). Put your trust in God- "Whatever time I am afraid, I will trust in thee. In God I will praise his word, in God I have put my trust; I will *not fear what flesh can do unto me"* (Psalm 56:3-4, KJV). When your needs overwhelm you, remember, your finite needs are nothing compared to God's infinite resources. Paul experienced and declared, "And my God will meet all your needs according to the riches of his glory in Christ Jesus" (Philippians 4:19, NIV).

4. **Fear to overcome challenges in life.** You have already overcome through God, who is already in you. "You are of God, little children, and have overcome them because He who is in you is greater than he who is in the world" (1 John 4:4, NKJV). This scripture tells you that as a leader, you belong to God. You, therefore, have already

CHAPTER 3
DEVELOPING COURAGE–BRAVERY

overcome the world because the One inside you, is greater than the ones around you—Satan and his agents—and in the world. Fear is not of God. God gives not the spirit of fear but that of power and love and a sound mind (2 Timothy 1:7) and of adoption and close intimacy. "For ye have not received the spirit of bondage again to fear; but ye have received the Spirit of adoption, whereby we cry, Abba, Father" (Romans 8:15, KJV). The Lord is your helper "for he hath said, I will never leave thee, nor forsake thee. So that we may boldly say, The Lord is my helper, and I will not fear what man shall do unto me "(Hebrews 13:5-6, KJV)

5. **Sense of fear for God's wrath for un-confessed sin.** "If My people, who are called by My name, will humble themselves and pray and seek My face and turn from their wicked ways, then will I hear from heaven and will forgive their sins and will heal their land" (II Chronicles 7:14). The conditions and responsibilities for this promise are for us to humble ourselves, pray to God and seek his face; seeking his face requires intense pursuit to find him since our sins hide us from His face; In His presence then, we must confess and repent of those sins. We are not allowed to cover our sins if we must prosper.

6. **Fear of condemnation from others or guilt**. Those who God has forgiven are forgiven indeed. "There is therefore now no condemnation to those (leaders) who are in Christ Jesus) who do not walk according to the flesh, but according to the Spirit. (Romans 8:1–2, NKJV). The sense of condemnation will paralyze our ability to come close to God and it makes us feel unworthy and it comes against our son-ship in God. If indeed, you have repented and confessed your sins, then believe that God has forgiven you. Fear comes from allowing the guilt and shame of the past to condemn us. This promise says if you are in Christ and have made sure that your sins are confessed, and you have repented of them; God will instantly forgive you and cleanse you from all unrighteousness. He has also promised that He would not remember them anymore. Forgive yourself then, turn to a new page, and work toward victory.

7. **Fear and need for guidance**. Leader-Servants need constant guidance from the Lord to lead. After all, the mission is His, and only He knows the best path to follow, as He declared: "Let everyone who is godly pray to You while You may be found…I will

instruct you and teach you in the way you should go; I will counsel you and watch over you" (Psalm 32:6, 8); understand that Bravery comes from Inward Peace: "Peace I leave with you, my peace *I give unto you: not as the world giveth, give I unto you. Let not your heart be troubled, neither let it be afraid"* (John 14:27, KJV).

8. **Fear and anxiety from worries**. Because the Heavenly Father knows what you need even before you ask for it, the leader's attitude to anxiety is to "Seek first His (Christ's) kingdom and His righteousness, and all things (food, drink, and clothing) will be given to you as well." Therefore, do not worry about tomorrow, for tomorrow will worry about itself" (Matthew 6:33–34, NIV). Cast all your cares upon the Lord because He cares for you (1 Peter 5:7). A leader must hold on to the fact that "In all things, God works for the good of those who love him, who have been called according to his purpose" (Romans 8:28, NIV).

9. **Fear from inadequate wisdom and confidence to move forward**. Leader-Servants are always faced with challenges beyond their natural wisdom. In those times, they face the fear of failure from inadequacy. They need God's supernatural power and wisdom. "If any of you lacks wisdom, he should ask God, who gives generously to all without finding fault, and it will be given to him. However, when he asks, he must believe and not doubt, because he who doubts is double-minded; understand that self-confidence encourages bravery. "But I would ye should understand, brethren, that the things which happened unto me have fallen out rather unto the furtherance of the gospel; So that my bonds in Christ are manifest in all the palace, and in all other places; And many of the brethren in the Lord, waxing confidence by my bonds, are much bolder to speak the word without fear" (Philippians 1:12-14, KJV).

10. **Fear of battling with temptation and sin against God.** "Submit yourself, then, to God. Resist the devil and he will flee from you" (James 4:7). Always remember Paul's words that "No temptation has seized you except what is common to man. And God is faithful; He will not let you be tempted beyond what you can bear. And when you are tempted, He will also provide a way out so that you can stand up under it" (1 Corinthians 10:13). Our attitude must always be to find a way to escape temptations by studying the Word of God and not dwell on any habits the lead us to fail God.

CHAPTER 3
DEVELOPING COURAGE–BRAVERY

11. **Fear of defeat in warfare.** The weapons of your warfare are divine power from God - not from you. As we are reminded by Paul, **"For the weapons of our warfare (fight) are not carnal but mighty in God for pulling down strongholds, casting down arguments and every high thing that exalts itself against the knowledge of God, bringing every thought into captivity to the obedience of Christ"** (II Corinthians 10:4–5 NKJV). Understand that God will not set you up to be ashamed, but He will give you victory if you follow His ways. *"Fear not; for thou shalt not be ashamed: neither be thou confounded; for thou shalt not be put to shame: for thou shalt forget the shame of thy youth, and shalt not remember the reproach of thy widowhood anymore."* (Isaiah 54:4) *Understand that the battle you face as a servant of the Lord is the Lord's (2 Chronicles 20:14-15).*

CASE OF BRAVERY AGAINST FEAR

The case of bravery is an example of overcoming fear for Courage. Great leaders will obtain victories over the battles they face in leadership by identifying and defining each challenge they face as a war against their calling; they must understand the purpose and the associated enemies; understand the precarious stage of the war; and the weapons of warfare; concentrating on God rather than man or intellect for each battle plan; and be determined to finish strong. Victories are clearly demonstrated by leaders such as King Jehoshaphat, Moses, Joshua, and many others in the Bible. In the case of King Jehoshaphat, a multitude of three great armies/enemies from all sides assembled against King Jehoshaphat for war (II Chronicles 20:1–25). For the victory, King Jehoshaphat made total obedience to God's plan and agenda the highest priority and took the following seven steps to secure victory:

1. **His courage triumphed over his fears.** He first had to be courageous to triumph over his fears. He was terrified in the face of impending danger and felt potential failure or the possibility of defeat. However, he stayed calm and collected and did not let the fear paralyze him. This first act of courage enabled him to think clearly to take the next steps.

2. **He consulted with the Lord for inner strength**. By praying and fasting with the people and proclaiming a fast that involved all the people, he gained more confidence in the plan and became more courageous to push ahead.
3. **He patiently listened to God to make the vision clearer**. He waited and listened until he caught God's vision and knew what to do. He was humble enough to acknowledge their vulnerabilities and credited their strength to God.
4. **He consulted with the people to extend his influence**. He assessed the stages and identified and appointed key leaders for different fronts in the battle, including those to praise and worship God. He led the battle as a celebration of God's strength ahead of the impending victory.
5. **He integrated praise and worship into the battle plan**. As part of the plan for victory, King Jehoshaphat understood that when the Lord said, "The battle is not yours but God's that praise and worship to God was an important element in any walk with God and a plan to defeat fear and sustain his people's morale.
6. **He exercised full faith to paralyzing fear**. He did not waiver in His understanding of the battle plan, for the Lord told him earlier that the battle was His. Jehoshaphat only needed to be courageous. Here we see courage as not the absence of fear, but full faith in God's plan to overcome fear.
7. **He understood the fear of failure in faith**. King Jehoshaphat understood that the fear of failure in the war was a failure in the faith in the strength of God, for the battle was His. As King Jehoshaphat noted in his prayer to God, "Our God, will you not judge them? For we have no power to face this vast army that is attacking us. We do not know what to do, but our eyes are on you" (II Chronicles 20:12, NIV). Triumphing over fear through full faith is the beginning of victory in any "war" that any leader will face.

Think about these seven steps and follow a similar model when you are faced with challenges and need to be courageous. Whatever the source of your fear might be, understand that fear is a paralyzing and controlling weapon against the authority of a leader.

SUMMARY 3
DEVELOPING COURAGE–BRAVERY

Before starting this exercise, please read and follow the instruction in the preface of this workbook. Answers to these questions are contained in this chapter. Completion of these exercises after reading the chapter should take 60-90 minutes.

Discovering the Acts of Courage-Bravery Attribute

1. Define courage-bravery attribute. Why as bravery the first critical act of courage
2. What does the Bible teach about fear? (II Timothy 1:7).
3. What are some of your personal sources of fear?

Understanding the Principle of Acts of Courage-bravery

1. Overcoming the paralyzing effects of fear is the weapons and tools a leader can use to overcome the challenges of fear as Principle #9: "Walking with God gives us the courage to overcome fear." [10] where does the bravery for overcoming fear come from?
2. Whatever the source of your fear might be, understand that fear is a paralyzing and controlling weapon against the authority of a leader.

Practicing the Acts of Courage-Bravery Attributes

Courage Bravery: The courage and audaciousness of overcoming the fear that paralyzes your courageous leadership or ability to take purposeful action; being open to direction and change.

1. What meaning or lesson can you frame from the experience of reading this chapter?
2. How can you display the act of bravery in the face of challenges?
3. What would you consider the most important characteristics of Courage and Bravery in the life of Young David?
4. How would you define your success? What choices are you willing to make?

5. Developing bravery in courage as an attitude starts by developing personal strategies to overcome fear. What are Acts of courage-bravery in these examples:
   a. Trust God as your tower of safety (Psalm 18:2,10; Matthew 7:25).
   b. Increase the presence of the Lord to cast away fear. (Matthew 11:28 NIV). (Psalm 91:1-5).
   c. Take safety and bravery in the promises of God. (Isaiah 62:6–7 NKJV). Faith is the building block of a leader's inner strength. (2 Peter 1:3-4).
6. Study the 12 Inner Strength Promises to Overcome Fear. I identify the conditions, the leaders acts, for the those promises .
7. Case of Bravery against Fear is an example of overcoming fear for Courage demonstrated by biblical leaders. In the case of King Jehoshaphat, a multitude of three great armies/enemies from all sides assembled against King Jehoshaphat for war (II Chronicles 20:1–25). For the victory, King Jehoshaphat made total obedience to God's plan and agenda the highest priority.
   a. What were his seven steps or acts of courage to secure victory?
   b. Think about these seven steps and follow a similar model when you are faced with challenges and need to be courageous.

CHAPTER 4
DEVELOPING COURAGE–STRENGTH

Courage-strength is the spiritual strength needed to build courage, initiate courageous action, or take the first stand in pursuing new ideas, building confidence in yourself and others. How do the people you lead see you in the face of challenges? Do they see fear? Or do they see courage displayed as inner strength? Here are a few examples of actions you can take to model courage that others can follow:

DEVELOP A SENSE OF INNER STRENGTH

Understanding and showing that God is the source of your strength is the beginning of overcoming the fear that paralyzes courage. God shows in (Deuteronomy 31:6 KJV): "Be strong and of a good courage, fear not, nor be afraid of them: for the LORD thy God, he is that doth go with thee; he will not fail thee, nor forsake thee" that the strength is from Him. To be strong in this context is more than physical strength with weapons. It is bold action and spiritual strength. Fear is an emotion of flesh that is always at its weak ends. Hence, the pathway to being strong is the ability to self-regulate your emotion and build spiritual fortitude. This is the case that Jesus faced in the Garden of Gethsemane (Matthew 26:36-46). He sought inner strength from the Lord for the agony of his impending death on the cross. He says, "My soul is overwhelmed with sorrow to the point of death. Stay here and keep watch with me" (Matthew 26: 37). In response, "He fell with his face to the ground and prayed, "My Father, if it is possible, may this cup be taken from me. Yet not as I will, but as you will" (Matthew 26:37-39). Jesus demonstrates here that to build inner strength for courage that overcomes fear; you must watch and pray, and not faint. He also sustained his strength by his self-will to be obedient to the Father's will.

DEVELOP STRENGTH FROM GOD'S PROMISES

Leading others by showing in your actions that God will not forsake you but will be with you to finish the work builds an inner strength to go on. It is comforting and reassuring for a leader who works with God to know and show that God will be with him and those he leads until the work is finished. Jesus is empowering us as His disciples say, "Go therefore and make disciples of all the nations, baptizing them in the name of the Father and the Son and the Holy Spirit, teaching them to observe all that I commanded you; and lo, I am with you always, even to the end of the age"(Matthew 28:19-20, NKJV). The Lord shall be with us, to guide and strengthen us, and bring us to safety in life issues of our day, till the end of the age. David's passing instruction to Solomon his son was to be "Be strong and of good courage, and do it: fear not, nor be dismayed: for the LORD God, even my God, will be with thee; he will not fail thee, nor forsake thee, until thou hast finished all the work for the service of the house of the LORD" (Chronicles 28:20, KJV). This was David encouraging his son Solomon to understand that God will sustain him until the end, but he must be spiritually strong and courageous. How are you encouraging those you lead?

DEVELOP INNER STRENGTH TO SUSTAIN COURAGE

Courage measures inner strength as strength builds and sustains courage. Although your inner spiritual strength is the catalyst that initiates courage, the audacious acts of courage of a leader who hopes in the Lord in the face of challenges sustain that strength. The Bible says, *"Be of good courage, and he shall strengthen your heart, all ye that hope in the LORD"* (Psalm 31:24, KJV). Understand that your strength is sustained by God's righteousness through His presence and His acts of holding you in his own hands as He has promised in these words: "Fear thou not; for I am with thee: be not dismayed; for I am thy God: I will strengthen thee; yea, I will help thee; yea, I will uphold thee with the right hand of my righteousness (Isaiah 41:10-13, KJV).

One of the attributes I have observed among leaders in mission fields is their ability to face their fears and needs by challenging their sense of comfort. Most successful people often are afraid of losing

Chapter 4
Developing Courage–Strength

their sense of comfort or those things they hold dear. This explains why there is a high rate of stress and emotional breakdown even suicide among the rich in times of financial crashes in which they lost their investments. You can also build courage from strength by the following:

1. **Be humble to listen to your critics but be bold to stand on your conviction –** Be bold to create an opportunity for open communication and exchange of ideas, yes, even from your critics. It is good to keep your friends close but be very informative to keep your enemies and critics even closer.

2. **Act with convictions without fear even when it is unpopular -** blunt *Bravery* and conviction in your vision-method *without fear* of pain is a key to displaying inner strength that builds courage.

3. **Display accountability.** Model accountability of yourself to your followers. A leader that holds people accountable for not following through is an important act of boldness and strength; it displays courage in leadership

4. **Let your message be direct and purposeful-** like in the case of John the Baptist; your message must be direct and purposeful in its content. Courageous leaders like John are often straight-talkers, readily sharing decision-making and accepting the sense that they do not have all the answers. Conflict and different perspectives may be expected, but intended content must be delivered as a display of courage.

5. **Lead and Initiate changes that will impact the lives of followers.** Leadership is primarily about serving to positively influence the lives of others as a pathway to the growth of an organization. Leading such a vision increases the strength and credibility of the leader as a change agent. The courage from such strength comes from the positive outcome of such initiation, even when you face challenges right from the start. It can also come from a leader's fortitude to engage all stakeholders in the change process.

6. **Expect and welcome resistance to change-** use constructive criticism as a positive aspect of diverse perspectives. Such attitude helps to innovate and reinforce the strength of a diverse team

WALK WITH GOD TO DEVELOP SPIRITUAL STRENGTH

The nine principles of spiritual leadership in servant-hood ministry provide guidelines for what walking with God can mean to a Leader-Servant. These include love and personal relationships, personal growth, faith, perseverance, courage, unbroken fellowship, spiritual transformation, submissive obedience, servant-hood, and courage over fear and are summarized below:

1. **Principle # 1: Walking with God means having a personal relationship with Him.** Walking with God is taking steps alongside God and having an intimate, personal relationship with Him. That relationship is based on the love of the Father (John 3:16) and faith that comes by hearing the word of God (Romans 10:17)

2. **Principle # 2: Walking with God is maintaining an unbroken fellowship with Him.** Maintaining fellowship means ensuring that the relationship is healthy with no barriers often due to un-confessed sin.

3. **Principle # 3: Walking with God is submissive obedience to His ways.** David walked with God and based on that experience; he advised his son Solomon before he died to be strong and to walk in the ways of God by keeping God's statutes and commandments in his judgments (1 Kings 2:23). Your courage and success in leadership depend on how much you know about the God that you serve through His word.

4. **Principle # 4: Walking with God requires perseverance to focus, on the unfinished tasks ahead-** Perseverance is being determined to walk with endurance, regardless of the circumstances.

5. **Principle # 5: Walking with God is faith measured by your works and your level of obedience.** A leader without a strong application of active faith in God's agenda, and what he believes, will have a weak starting point for leadership and perhaps a poor ending. Active faith is a faith with works without a doubt.

6. **Principle # 6: Walking with God produces growth through deeper knowledge and experience.** - remain focused and recognize that

suffering through persecution is to be expected in their chosen walk with God.

7. **Principle # 7: Walking with God transforms our mind to know the perfect will of God.** We are to focus our thoughts on things that are true, honest, just, pure, lovely, and things of good report ((Romans 12:2; Philippians. 4:8).

8. **Principle # 8: Walking with God is an act of servant-hood whereby we emulate Jesus** through selfless service to others motivated by our love and humility (Matthew 20:26-27).

9. **Principle # 9: Walking with God gives us the courage to overcome fear.** Fear is the devil's primary weapon of war against a Leader-Servant. Peter's vulnerability while walking on the water toward Jesus was fear.

SUMMARY 4
DEVELOPING COURAGE–STRENGTH

Before starting this exercise, please read and follow the instruction in the preface of this workbook. Answers to these questions are contained in this chapter. Completion of these exercises after reading the chapter should take 60-90 minutes.

Discovering the Acts of Courage-Strength

Define Courage-strength. How do the people you lead see you in the face of challenges?

Understanding the Principle of Acts of Courage Strength

1. How can the following nine principles of walk with God develop spiritual strength
    a. Having a personal relationship with Him
    b. Maintaining an unbroken fellowship with Him.
    c. Submissive obedience to His ways.
    d. Perseverance to focus, on the unfinished tasks ahead-
    e. Faith measured by your works and your level of obedience.
    f. produces growth through deeper knowledge and experience. -
    g. Transforms our mind to know the perfect will of God.

      h. An act of servant-hood whereby we emulate Jesus
      i. Gives us the courage to overcome **fear.**

Practicing the Acts of Courage Strength

1. **Courage-Strength** is the spiritual strength needed to build courage, initiate courageous action, or take the first stand in pursuing new ideas, building confidence in yourself and others
2. What meaning or lesson can you frame from the experience of reading this chapter?
3. How can you lead people in the face of challenges? Do they see fear? Or do they see courage displayed as strength?
4. How can you show that God is your strength and will not fail you?
5. How can your Spiritual Strength Comes from Walking with God?
6. A sense of inner strength to overcome fear is developed by Understanding and showing that God is the source of your strength.
    a. What did God show in (Deuteronomy 31:6 KJV) that the strength is from Him?
    b. What does "to be strong" mean in this context?
7. The pathway to being strong is the ability to self-regulate your emotion and build spiritual fortitude. How did Jesus demonstrate this in Garden of Gethsemane (Matthew 26:36-46)?
8. How is the Act of Courage Strength developed from God's promises? (see Chronicles 28:20, KJV).
    a. What was David purpose in this instruction?
    b. How are you encouraging those you lead?
9. How does courage measures inner strength as strength builds and sustains courage?. *(see* Psalm 31:24, KJV.
10. How do you build courage from strength?

CHAPTER 5
DEVELOPING COURAGE– SELF-WILL

Courage-self-will involve self-leadership, and self-determination for building confidence in yourself and others; it requires self-regulation of your emotions and exercise of faith in people. How does self-will display a leader's inner strength and ability to take a stand on an issue without fear? Here are a few examples:

Develop the will for self-determination

Most courageous leaders demonstrate the will for self-determination to persevere, even in a history of past failures. When one considers the self-will and perseverance of Abraham Lincoln and all other leaders that suffered periods of failures before they succeeded, one can come up with one clear conclusion—courage can be born of self-will. These leaders did not fear the humiliation of another failure; they just persevered until the end. In self-leadership, regulating your emotion toward successes and failures equips you to take a stand on an issue without fear of losing control when challenged. It is usually a display of poor leadership when we see leaders get involved in quarrels or exchange vulgarities in responding to hurtful situations. Such leaders simply look like kids who need some sense of direction. Emotional self-regulation is an important dimension of self-leadership. It is the capacity to regulate and control one's emotions to channel attention to the good of another person. (See the full discussion in *Leadership Empathy Attribute in Authentic Leader as Servant Part I*). Self-regulation involves the self-will to enter into and walk through another person's emotional state; it also requires us to learn and understand how we can relate to others by adjusting our behavior. How can self-regulation display courageous leadership? Here are a few examples:

Display courage from self-awareness-A leader having an understanding of what can anger him/her will have the ability to improve his or her self-control and responses to issues. Our awareness (not ignorance) of the devices of the enemy equips us to better handle the devil's subtleties intended to draw us into ungodliness. Such ability usually builds a sense of courage to take a stand against the enemy. In the presence of uncertainties in an unfamiliar situation, increased emotional capacity is a required asset in courageous leadership to lead people through difficulties.

Display courage to channel your emotions directly to God. Courageous leaders like Moses, David, and Joshua expressed their needs and feelings directly to God without fear, as they found comfort and strength from the promises of God.

Display courage in expressing feelings to God. Even though leaders can regulate their emotions, courageous leaders can express their feeling in a decision and display a sense of self-security and confidence in people in expressing their feelings to the leader.

Display courage from the correct perception of yourself. How one perceives him/herself often determines self-esteem, self-confidence, courage to take action, and attitude in several aspects of life. If you perceive yourself as a child of God, your attitude in the face of challenges will reflect the courage to overcome fear over the situation.

Display courage from an ability to lead others-Correct perception of yourself increases your courage from your ability to lead others; positive perception and self-efficacy allow you the ability to identify those things you want to change or improve. Leaders who display an ability to lead others are very self-secure and usually are good at self-reflective listening; they are very authentic and readily accept both mistakes and successes, and give credit to followers. The courage to take a stand comes from their understanding and using their personal value system to influence change.

Display courage from purpose-driven life. Self-regulation is a product of self-leadership, leaders have a better quality of spiritual life and the capacity to take charge of their lives by focusing on what matters most, and the change that they influence. Attitudes are best driven by their value system, their motivation in love to serve, and their commitment to inspiring behavioral change in others.

Display courage from effective Communication – Communicating courageously results from the leader's ability to self-regulate his or her emotions in order to lead and communicate effectively with others without fear. Being able to self-regulate your emotion to build character and respect increases the leader's ability to challenge the wrong in others as he or she also acknowledges and corrects his or her own mistakes.

CHAPTER 5
DEVELOPING COURAGE–SELF-WILL

Modeling a good example gives the leader the moral capital and courage to correct others without the fear of others questioning your authority and leadership in the change you are expecting in them

SUMMARY 5
DEVELOPING COURAGE–SELF-WILL

Before starting this exercise, please read and follow the instruction in the preface of this workbook. Answers to these questions are contained in this chapter. Completion of these exercises after reading the chapter should take 60-90 minutes

Discovering the Acts of Courage Self-will

1. What are the elements of courage-self-will?
2. What are some examples of how self-will displays a leader's inner strength and ability to take a stand on an issue without fear?

Practicing the Acts of Courage self-will

Courage-Self- Will involves self-leadership and self-determination for building confidence in yourself and others; it requires self-regulation of your emotions and the exercise of faith in people.

1. What meaning or lesson can you frame from the experience of reading this chapter?
2. How does self-will display a leader's ability to take a stand on an issue without fear?
3. How can you be Self-determined to persevere, even in a history of past failures?
4. In developing the will for self-determination in the life of , how can courage can be born of self-will
5. How can self-regulation display courageous leadership? Fill in the blanks:
   a) Display courage from _____ self-awareness-
   b) Display courage to channel your _____ to God.
   c) Display courage in expressing _____ to God.
   d) Display courage from the correct _____
   e) Display courage from an _____ to lead others
   f) Display courage from A _____ life.
   g) Display courage from effective _____

CHAPTER 6
DEVELOPING COURAGE–
DECISIVENESS

Courage-decisiveness is the last stage of courageous leadership. It is the ability to readily and openly make tough decisions without fear of critics on uncomfortable challenging issues, and opposite opinions. Decisiveness is a characteristic of responsibility attribute. How does decisiveness display courage and evidenced in a leader's ability to take a stand on an issue without fear? Here are a few examples:

DEVELOP A SENSE OF QUICKNESS TO ACT ON ISSUES

Other than the display of inner strength, decisiveness is the second most important element of courageous leadership, as it is the beginning of the outward result of courageous leadership. Decisiveness can be measured by our sense of urgency and quickness to act on critical issues that matter. Taking a stand is a direct product of decisiveness, especially when the issue, for whatever reason, is not agreed to by all stakeholders. When there is fear of possible failure, some leaders will analyze the options and fail to make a decision because of fear. A preacher once described it as a 'paralysis of analyses.

Readily making an instinctive decision that builds courage is a mark of courageous leadership. Decisive courage can be displayed by making a decision following your own instinct and conviction, even when several odds point in the opposite direction. A decision based on minority conviction is a measure of courage. In such cases, such a decision is a risk that if it fails, could be construed as a failure of leadership by critics. However, most great leaders and successful entrepreneurs are master risk-takers, as they often create growth opportunities from the ability to take and manage risks.

In my early years as a diversity dean, I inherited an affirmative action program that had been in existence for over 30 years. It was clear to many that the program had not worked well in the current culture, and was in fact setting students up for failure. Most people would want the program to be replaced or discontinued but feared a backlash from the alumni community; no one was willing to risk being labeled by this very outspoken community. I was convinced that we could do better without this program. After a serious analysis of the program structure and outcomes, I took a stand to design a better program and obtained the initial funding to initiate a new program. I made the unthinkable decision to discontinue the old program, replacing it with the new program, in name and content. Yes, it angered the alumni, but a few years later; they all came on board as they saw that the new program was yielding positive and better outcomes.

DEVELOP BOLDNESS TO CONFRONT ISSUES

The critical responsibility of top executives is influencing change not only in the desired direction of people but also in the organization. One of the expected challenges is confronting key performance factors such as hiring, firing, or reassigning people. Confronting the issues of people or units of the organization not performing skillfully and making the right decision can be daunting and often very frustrating. In some organizations, especially in public institutions, firing a staff, even when the staff is not performing well, is so difficult that you have to be creative to be legally successful. It takes courage to confront such issues.

Hiring new staff is expensive and time-consuming just as firing an unproductive staff can also be stressful and frustrating. Taking from the Biblical exhortation to be at peace with all men whenever and wherever possible, can be daunting in confronting performance issues; especially when considering reassigning unproductive staff rather than firing them. A great leader will rather retain, cast a new vision, improve communication, and set performance goals with clear standards rather than quick termination of unproductive staff. Thus, one key courageous strategy for confronting human performance issues is effective communication. Here are a few decisiveness courage strategies:

Humbly connect and relate to the follower before confrontation for correction. This is a clear standard that God set for humanity. He created an opportunity for man to connect and relate to Him and has no pleasure in the death of a sinner. It is a mark of courage for a leader to first exhaust time to bring an unproductive staff member or follower up to the expected standard before any move for termination or even admonishment. In the book of Malachi, we learnt how Prophet Malachi served the people of God during a period of intense corruption and wicked practices of priests and leaders, who compromised the word of God with a false sense of security with God. Malachi is a good case study of confronting human performance factors through effective communication that focuses first on connecting to the follower. "Leaders earn the right to change the life of their followers by first affirming their identity and relationship to the leader" [15] following the process of (Malachi 1:2-14)

1. Looking first for the good of the follower
2. Identifying what he can affirm in the follower.
3. Being specific about what needs to be affirmed by the leader.
4. Being specific about what needs to be changed in the follower.
5. Challenging the follower to grow through change and self-leadership.
6. Commutating to the follower why the change is important.
7. Expressing confidence that the followers can change if they make an effort.
8. Setting goals and standards that will measure the service excellence, and walk with God.

A CASE STUDY OF COURAGE FOR GOOD SUCCESS

The definition of success is an abstract idea in our today's society because people define success relative to some aspect of sense or feeling of success (spiritual, physical, emotional, educational, vocational, and financial). Whichever way you choose to define success will depend on what your purpose is in life and what you value most. Let me explain this case example.

Walking down one of the busiest streets in the city of New Orleans, which can be true for any busy street of any modern city, I watched as people of all races, statures, nationality, and gender, etc.

race through the street in cars or walk along the busy sidewalk. I tried to make sense of or think of one thing that these people had in common. They could be racing to work to make a living, to school to pursue an education to improve their quality of life, to enjoy a quiet vacation time of rest after a busy year, going to the casino to gamble to win a fortune, to church for worship to serve God more, or just going to the gym for physical health. I concluded that every one of these people wants one thing in common— success in whatever thing for which they are racing. Each of them must have a different definition of what that success is or the map to complete the journey. And then I thought; could there be one definition of success that could fit every situation or journey to success? In that journey and sea of successes, we have enjoyed the achievements of people who have been successful— inventions of the automobile, the creation of the telephone, medical discoveries that led to the control of many diseases, the invention of computers and the internet, great leaders like General George Patton, President Abraham Lincoln or success symbols like Bill Gate and Isaac Newton. So, I asked myself, as I tried to make more sense out of what appeared to be a state of chaos, what is a good or true success and how could a leader achieve it and yet have trust credibility?

To the rich young ruler in the Bible, success is a material possession rather than love for his neighbor. In general, success is the achievement of something desired, planned, or attempted; success reflects a destination; to get to a destination, you need to have a plan on how to get there. Success, like a destination, can be mapped out with a linear or non-linear path. Some may fear failures on the way, but most successful leaders are able to overcome their fears. One principle to remember is this: *If you plan with clarity and purpose, you will surely arrive safely at your destination!* Success is a direct result of your habit, which is shaped by behaviors and choices in life. Most flourishing leaders have what I call a *success habit*— positive behavior and making positive choices toward success.

Success in general is different from 'good success' which is the natural opposite of failure. Before we posit a functional definition of *good success*, we need to agree that there are many notable people who have succeeded after their initial failures. What were the common characteristics of their successes? Consider the following short list

CHAPTER 6
DISPLAYING COURAGE–DECISIVENESS

that spans different works in the lives of people that have had credible successes in life:

- Winston Churchill struggled in school and failed the sixth grade. After school, he faced many years of political failures; in fact, he was defeated in every election for public office until he was finally twice-elected Prime Minster of the United Kingdom and Nobel Prize-winner. [17]
- Abraham Lincoln started his life, especially his youth with several failures. He went to war as a captain and returned demoted to a private. Lincoln failed in almost anything he started in his early life. He started numerous failed businesses and was defeated in his several runs for public office. However, today, Lincoln is remembered as one of the greatest presidents and leaders of the United States. [18]
- Harry S. Truman started life with few failures of his own and few wrong choices. He started a store that sold silk shirts, and other clothing. The company soon failed and went bankrupt a few years later. Truman afterward found success as a WWI vet, Senator, Vice President, and eventually President of the United States. [18]
- While Albert Einstein is synonymous with genius, he was a failure in his early endeavors; he did not speak until he was four and did not read until he was seven. His teachers and even his parents thought he was mentally handicapped, slow, and anti-social. Einstein was eventually expelled from school and was refused admittance to the Zurich Polytechnic School. Nevertheless, this drop-out caught a vision, and with confidence went on to win the Nobel Prize for his contributions to modern physics. [20]
- Isaac Newton had some failures early in life. He never did very well in school and failed when he was positioned to manage and run the family farm. He failed so miserably that an uncle took charge and sent him off to Cambridge, where he finally caught up and became successful; today he is an internationally well-known scholar. [21]
- In his early businesses, Henry Ford failed financially five times before he founded the successful Ford Motor Company. [22]
- Thomas Edison was told by his teachers that he was too stupid to learn anything; he was fired from his first two jobs for not being

productive enough. Later, as an inventor, Edison made 1,000 unsuccessful attempts at inventing the light bulb before his failures resulted in the design that worked. [23]
- Bill Gates dropped out of Harvard and failed in his first business with Microsoft's co-founder Paul Allen. Gates did not give up and his later attempt created a global empire that is the organization known as Microsoft. [24]
- Early in life, Oprah Winfrey endured a rough and abusive childhood. She has also endured numerous career setbacks, including being fired from her job as a television reporter because she was "unfit for TV." Today, Oprah is one of the most iconic faces on television as well as one of the richest and most successful women in the world. She is also a person who did not allow failure to define her destiny; a woman who started with failure and ended with success. [25]

What do all these people have in common? None had any direct mentor or inherited any fortune from their parents, but they all eventually succeeded. What exactly propelled them to turn their failures into eventual success? All of them have trust credibility and a positive reputation. I believe that your ultimate success in life is a destination with several intentional successful steps while going through a number of challenges. In that context, your failure is only a challenge or setback in one of those steps but does not define your ultimate success or destination. It is not difficult to see that each of these people had four self-leadership characteristics in common. We posit that for most prosperous people, success is a journey; it is a combination of success habits of self-will, self-confidence, self-determination, and perseverance:

- **Self-will to succeed.** They all had self-will and determination to succeed. Think about Abraham Lincoln. How could a man who was demoted from captain to the lowest rank, private, rise to become the president of the greatest nation on earth? It was not luck. Growing up and raising my children, I have always told them that memories of the past create aspirations for success or failure depending on one's perspective. If you focus on failure, you will be too paralyzed by fear to move forward. If you respond to the failure by searching only for the *why* you failed, ignoring the *where* and *how*, you will miss the opportunity to learn from the failure, to refocus your vision and energy toward a strategy for success.

- **Self-confidence in themselves to succeed.** Most successful people believe in themselves and that they can achieve their goals. They had self-awareness and a deep sense that they had the talent for what they were pursuing, no matter the assessments of others. They desired to prove themselves right. Memories of past failures create aspiration for success only when you focus on success through self-will and self-confidence in your personal values to succeed no matter what it takes. It means refusing to accept the initial failure not as the endpoint, but instead as a bump on the road that redirects success—a bigger success. It means seeing failure as a natural path of a journey toward greatness.
- **Self-determination to succeed.** These people were very competitive and determined by their own will, choice, and initiative to change their current position. *Fred Thorlin, a one-time director of APX, recalled his encounter with Bill Gate in an interview,* "I showed him a simple game which you could play in well under a minute. I beat him in about 35 out of 37 efforts. I came back a month later; he won or tied every game. He had studied the game until he solved it. That is a competitor. "[25] These people had no problem with self-esteem; rather, they were so confident and self-determined that they could nurture their talent to greatness.
- **Perseverance over the challenges to succeed.** They all had the perseverance to continue until their goals were met. The assertion below is about Lincoln as a good leader who exemplified these four principles of self-will, self-confidence, self-determination, and perseverance. Consider the following account:

At the age of seven, a young boy and his family were forced out of their home. The boy had to work to support his family. At the age of nine, his mother passed away. When he grew up, the young man was keen on going to law school but had no education.

At 22, he lost his job as a store clerk. At 23, he ran for state legislature and lost. The same year, he went into business. It failed, leaving him with a debt that took him 17 years to repay.

At 27, he had a nervous breakdown. Two years later, he tried for the post of speaker in his state legislature. He lost. At 31, he was defeated in his attempt to become an elector. By 35, he was defeated twice while running for Congress. Finally, he did manage to secure a brief term in Congress, but at 39, he lost his re-election bid.

At 41, his four-year-old son died. At 42, he was rejected as a prospective land officer. At 45, he ran for the Senate and lost. Two years later, he lost the vice-presidential nomination. At 49, he ran for Senate and lost again.

At 51, he was elected the President of the United States of America.

The man in question: is Abraham Lincoln.
**** *Author unknown*

Do you see the magnitude of failures and misfortunes in Lincoln's life? However, he never gave up. He did not allow those failures to define his success. Abraham Lincoln could have had all the attributes we discussed in this book. Without self-will, self-confidence, self-determination, and perseverance added to these attributes, he would not have been able to turn his series of failures and misfortunes into success. Note that some of the failures were not of his making and were outside his control. Nevertheless, excuses were not an option for him.

I believe that self-will as an element of self-leadership is the greatest mentor to turn failure into credible success. Self-will is the primary driver for determination and perseverance. It is what wakes one up in the morning to ask for strength to do God's will. However, the notion that people, in general, can succeed after their initial failures can be misleading in comparison to someone who lacks the skills or self-will for the next step to achieve the desired success in life. The proponents of this myth argue that having enough confidence can propel failure to success. I argue that to reposition oneself from a failed attempt to success, one needs more than self-confidence. No amount of confidence-building through mentoring will compensate for a lack of self-will along with the basic skills or talent on which to build future attempts. Even if that person has the IQ of a genius, self-will is needed to channel actions to success. Indeed, over-confidence without self-will to acquire and build basic skills can set that person up for failure and the profound destruction of the person's self-esteem.

CHAPTER 6
DISPLAYING COURAGE–DECISIVENESS

BRAVERY MODEL FOR GOOD SUCCESS

Obviously, the people in the list above had success with worldly inner values in God's eyes. They were all successful in excellent things through well-applied choices. However, the Bible differentiates success with an internal value from good success with eternal value. We also have bad successes, that is when you are successful at the wrong things—the bad and evil things. People have made millions from bad music or movies, some of which feed into the devil's destructive plan. Others became wealthy by stealing, cheating, and defrauding the system or others. These are not good successes and are very temporary and never bring the joy of eternal good success. Many years ago, even as a graduate student, I received a letter from my mother, saying, "Son, look at your mates. Some are driving more than six cars and building big houses. When are you going to be successful like them?" I wrote back to my mother and asked her if she knew how those friends made the wealth. I assured her that I would be successful in God's time and purpose. Less than two years later, the same friend was caught stealing company funds and people's goods in his care. He was fired from the job. Today, he is financially broke with no reputation and credibility. Financial success by ill- means is not a good success and never yields trust credibility.

I post that *good success is the achievement of something that is of eternal value to God*. Only God is good, and good success must have an eternal value to this good God. The ordinary success of internal values such as those listed above, when out of love and obedience to God to serve others, could be considered a good success. The question is: Is there a rule or principle for good success that can be consistently applied with some guaranteed result in all areas of our lives? The simple answer is YES. The Biblical principles of success have been tested over thousands of years and proven to yield good results. We see through the Scriptures God's model for good success that needs to be desired by every leader or follower who aspires to be a great leader. The following could be considered examples of good success:

- Knowing the perfect will of God.
- Making sure that your soul is secured in God, death or alive.
- Walking with God in this life.

- Forgiveness and for your enemy.
- Humble enough to love and serve others.
- Winning the battle over worldliness.
- The excellence of the knowledge of Christ Jesus.
- Gaining the power of His resurrection and being found in Christ,
- Fellowship of His sufferings, being conformed to His death,
- Salvation and Eternal life.

Each of these good successes can also be part of a journey leading to other good successes or become your formula to lead to even greater good successes. For example, salvation from believing in Jesus leads to the ultimate prize of entering eternal life. Similarly, practicing forgiveness; whereby you release someone that hurts you can lead to prosperity and good blessings from God.

THE FORMULA FOR GOOD SUCCESS

We can identify the key elements of what a journey to good success entails in the lives of several Biblical leaders like Isaac, Moses, Joshua, Joseph, Daniel, Nehemiah, Paul, Jesus Christ, and others. Let us consider a few of these to frame our formula for good success:

Isaac's Formula: Walking with God, Covenant Promise, Self-will, Self-Regulation, and Perseverance. Isaac's Journey to good success began with an opportunity. He sowed in the time of famine but reaped a mighty harvest. God had promised to bless him and multiply his descendants "as the stars of heaven… because Abraham obeyed My voice and kept My charge, My commandments, My statutes, and My laws" (Genesis 26:4-5). He turned the famine into a growth opportunity; he sowed and God watered, and he became very prosperous because *God was in it*—God blessed the work of his hand in a drought (Genesis 26:13). It showed that when God is in your business, you will become very prosperous and have a good success.

Isaac was prepared for the pain and challenges of continued good success. The enemy did not want Isaac to prosper. In this case, the Philistines envied him and had stopped up all the wells which his father's servants had dug in the days of Abraham his father and had filled them with earth for they reasoned out of envy that he mightier than they were (Genesis 26:15-16). Isaac was also prepared for the external challenges of his good success. When the wells were filled up, and he was sent away, Isaac departed from there and pitched his tent in the Valley of Gerar, and dwelt there (Genesis 26:17-19). He made very *critical choices*: he moved without hesitation; he pitched his tent at Gerar and dwelt there. He did not try to force himself or rationalize remaining in the old place. Rather, Isaac repositioned himself for greater and more assured success; he tried a new location and expected a change. For new success, you must try a new approach. It is only a weakness that fears change; change is an element of a progressive organization.

Isaac was aware of the disputes and contentions but was *self-willed* and *self-determined* to overcome them. "Isaac's servants dug in the valley and found a well of running water there. However, the herdsmen of Gerar quarreled with Isaac's herdsmen, saying, "The water is ours". (Genesis 26:19-20). Isaac was successful in finding water, but the enemy took the water. He chose not to focus or be limited by the circumstances. He was self-willed and determined to overcome to reach his purposeful success. Isaac proved this principle: with God, you will succeed where your enemy has failed or think you will fail. Isaac *persevered*, though his opposition worked against his destined success. "Then they dug another well, and they quarreled over that *one* also. So he called its name Sitnah" (Genesis 26:21). The relentlessness of an enemy can be overcome by perseverance, and you cannot afford to give up. Isaac chose to persevere; he also chose to give up his right to the well.

Isaac *self-regulated* his emotions. With a focus on your mission, any opposition will bring you to your room for success (your Rehoboth), but you must persevere and choose to remain undaunted. Isaac controlled his emotions and moved from there and "dug another well, and they did not quarrel over it. So he called its name Rehoboth, because he said, "For now the LORD has made room for us, and we shall be fruitful in the land" (Genesis 26:22). Isaac in his journey and choices for success showed that when you reposition yourself and add God to your plan, He will show up to direct your success. You must know when not to contend with the opposition, but focus on the fact that good success is with God. Isaac did not quit his journey; he dug again and found water—his Rehoboth water.

Isaac's success begot greater success. If great good success is possible, then a small initial success is not enough. Isaac's Rehoboth was just the beginning of a greater Beersheba success. He showed that the Lord will make perfect everything that concerns a leader that walks with Him beyond the initial room for success. "Then he went up from there to Beersheba and there the LORD appeared to him: "do not fear, for I *am* with you. I will bless you and multiply your descendants ..." And there Isaac's servants dug a well..." (Genesis 26:23-25) and they found water again. Isaac built on and expanded his Rehoboth success to his Beersheba: the Well of 7 Oaths. What did Isaac find in his Beersheba? In addition to the water, he found a more intimate presence of God; he found peace with his oppositions; He found assured confidence and courage; and most importantly, he found good success and blessings of eternal value to God.

Moses' Formula: Submissive Obedience, Trust, Intimate walk with God. When God appeared to Moses to charge him for his journey of good success (to deliver Israel out of slavery in Egypt and lead them to the Promised Land), how did God equip him and what did he do with that equipment? God prepared and equipped Moses by directly revealing Himself to him like no other human being, and he *believed* the God that appeared to him. This was the first element in Moses' formula for good success. God said, "I *am* the God of your father—the God of Abraham, the God of Isaac, and the God of Jacob" (Exodus 3:6, NKJV), and Moses believed.

Second, Moses' *clear understanding* of the key elements of his journey— the possibility of rejection from Pharaoh, danger of being arrested and killed, the rejection of him, and the message by Israel themselves—was an important element of his formula. The message was clear though very daunting because Moses knew how powerful Egypt and Pharaoh could be. However, God said, "Come now; therefore, and I will send you to Pharaoh, that you may bring My people, the children of Israel, out of Egypt" (Exodus 3:10, NKJV). A clear understanding of a mission usually leads to the right perspective and vision for the journey.

The third element of his formula was that Moses not only believed and had a clear perspective of the journey; he *trusted* in this God, who also *convinced* him that he was the man for this great journey to the Promise Land of destiny. God said to Moses, "I will certainly be with you. "I AM WHO I AM…you shall say to the children of Israel" (Exodus 3:14-15 NKJV). He believed and used the power of this God, which was shown to him through his experience in the burning bush and all the signs, to increase his trust-confidence. He was assured that God would honor His word for God said, "I will stretch out My hand and strike Egypt with all My wonders which I will do in its midst" (Exodus 3:20, NKJV). Even when no one else could believe in the face of all odds, like when they arrived in front of the red sea, Moses trusted the LORD and commanded his followers, saying; "Stand still, and see the salvation of the LORD, which He will accomplish for you today. For the Egyptians whom you see today, you shall see again no more forever" (Exodus 14:13, NKJV). There, in front of them was the red sea, and behind and all around was the powerful Pharaoh and strong Egyptian army (Exodus 14: 15-19).

The fourth element of Moses' formula was his *intimacy* with God and *God's Presence*. God revealed to Moses His very special name, which He never revealed to others before him. He said, to Moses, "I *am* the LORD. I appeared to Abraham, to Isaac, and Jacob, as God Almighty, but *by* My name LORD, I was not known to them" (Exodus 6:2-3 NKJV). "The LORD spoke to Moses intimately as a man speaks to his friend" (Exodus 33:11). God was personal and told Moses that He knew him and had given him a favor. Moses used this assurance to request more grace for him and his people to be separate from other people: "I pray, if I have found grace in Your sight, show me now Your way, that I may know You and that I may find grace in Your sight. And consider that this nation *is* Your people" (Exodus 33:12-14, NKJV) This intimacy and God presence was so important to Moses' success that he told God that they would not continue unless God's presence continued with them (Exodus 33:15-16). In this sense, Moses knew this God more closely and God honored his request, and said, "My Presence will go *with you,* and I will give you rest…I will make all My goodness pass before you, and I will proclaim the name of the LORD before you."

And the fifth essential element of his success was his ability and *resilience* to speak and follow what God had commanded, "I have made you *as* God to Pharaoh… You shall speak all that I command you" (Exodus 7:1-2, NKJV). Moses trusted and believed in God so much that nothing mattered but to see the journey to the end. His journey had three primary and continuous stages: first; he must deliver Israel out of bondage from Egypt; second; he must lead them through the desert, and third; he must lead them to enter and settle in the Promised Land. Moses had good successes in the first and second stages, for "Israel saw the great work which the LORD had done in Egypt; so the people feared the LORD and believed the LORD and His servant Moses" (Exodus 14:31, NKJV) Unfortunately, Moses failed in the third stage of his journey because of disobedience.

In summary, Moses failed to reach his destined success for the Promised Land because of a wrong choice: poor self-mastery of his emotions; he became angry when the people became contentious and clouded his vision of what God wanted. Can you see yourself in that example? Not until Moses made the wrong choice and ignored the elements of trust and obedience in his journey for 'good success', he was doing all right. He saw the Promised Land but could not go in. Why? Here is a principle to summarize this: *If you can see it, you can reach it, but only with the right choices*! This principle was proven by Moses. God did not allow him to reach his destined good success simply because he made the wrong choice of disobeying Him and taking His glory for the water supply. Submissive obedience is the result of love and humility. If Moses had continued with his true faith in God and the love for Him with which he started, he would not have disobeyed God. He used God's power wisely but later saw the faith and power in himself more than it coming from God to bring water out of the rock. This is very true of today's leaders. Trust and focusing on God's ways with submissive obedience to Him are the most essential elements of our formula for good success that has eternal value to God.

Joshua's formula: Consistent resilience, strength, courage, and obedience in God's ways. God was clear to Joshua on what the secret of his success should be: Only be strong and very courageous, and absolutely obedient to God's word. God said, "This Book of the Law shall not depart from your mouth, but you shall *meditate* in it day and night, that you may *observe* to do according to all that is written in it. For then *you* will make your way prosperous, and then you will have *good success*" (Joshua 1:8). Working and using this formula, God said that he, Joshua, would make his way prosperous to the limit of his ability to obey God's ways, and then, he will achieve *good success*. This is self-leadership; he must lead himself in the journey of his expected success by making good key choices: he must add to his strength of character, courage, obedience, consistency in meditating on the word, and observing to do God's bidding in all matters. God's ways are His statutes, judgments, and commandments in His written Word; and Joshua did obey and had good success. Under Joshua's leadership, Israel reached and settled in the Promised Land, and the LORD gave rest to Israel from all their enemies roundabout. Joshua passed on his formula of good success to Israel in his farewell speech before he died:

> *So you shall possess their land, as the* LORD *your God promised you. Therefore, be very courageous to keep and to do all that is written in the Book of the Principle of Moses, lest you turn aside from it to the right hand or to the left...And you know in all your hearts and in all your souls that not one thing has failed of all the good things which the* LORD *your God spoke concerning you (Joshua 23:4-14, NKJV).*

King David's Formula: Consistent obedience, humility, repentance, trust, and walking in God's ways. King David's formula for success for his son, Solomon, was to keep the charge of God, walk in His ways, His statutes, His commandments, His judgments, and His testimonies for him to prosper in all that he did and wherever he turned (1 Kings 2:2, NKJV); he must not walk in the counsel of the ungodly, but must delight in the Principle of the LORD, keep and meditate on His law day and night so that whatever he does shall prosper. David's advice was based on his self-leadership experience in the journey to success. Solomon believed and knew that he had to trust in the LORD with all his heart, and must only lean on the understanding of the Lord, and not his own (Proverb 3:5, NKJV). Walking in God's ways means delighting in and following His statutes, judgments, and commandments in His written Word and leaning on your understanding of God's ways. It also means humility and readiness to repent and forsake sin against God and man. The Bible says, "He who covers his sins will not prosper. But whoever confesses and forsakes *them* will have mercy (Proverb 28: 13, NKJV). David modeled this principle very well and prospered, despite his sin, because he was humble enough to confess and ask for forgiveness. David understood, and we should also, that if walking with God is an element of our formula for success, then we could not allow sin to break our fellowship with God. We must confess our failures as part of the equation and move on with our walk with God.

As long as Solomon applied his Father, David's formula, he was successful. He found favor and *good success* in the sight of God and man (Proverbs 3:1-4, NKJV). He started failing when he deviated from it, a lesson for us leaders. However, he also found a formula using his self-leadership principles. He asked God: "Therefore give to Your servant an understanding heart to judge Your people, that I may discern between good and evil." God was pleased by this request and granted it, giving Solomon a wise and understanding heart, and added to his request, material prosperity. God also added long life for which Solomon did not ask, but under the express condition that he walked in obedience to His ways to keep His statutes and commandments (1 Kings 3:9, 14). Unfortunately, Solomon did not meet these conditions, and died too early; he failed in his leadership, showing the vital need for obedience to God as a critical element in any formula for good success, as was the case in Moses' example who failed eventually also.

Joseph's formula: Obedience to God, hard work, positive attitude, self-mastery. Joseph's formula for success was to walk in obedience to God added to the desire not to sin against God. He stands as an example of a leader who could turn his life challenges into incredible good success by following the simple formula of obedience, and his desire to follow God's ways. The Bible says, "The LORD was with Joseph, and he was a successful man... and whatever he did; the LORD made *it* prosper" (Genesis 39:2-3, NKJV). God being with Joseph was the key to his success. Regardless of the circumstances that came to Joseph's life, God turned them to his advantage for good success. Each challenge that Joseph faced was designed to discourage him. It did reinforce that all things work together for good to them that love God (Romans 8:28).

Joseph's *attitude and approach* to life were also key elements of his success. He had a *positive attitude* and *self-mastery* of his emotions that allowed him to let go of the past by *forgiving* his brothers and others that hurt him unjustly; he was diligent, hardworking, and faithful in the responsibilities set before him as a slave and a prisoner. With his forgiving heart, Joseph was at peace with himself, with those that set him up for failure, and most importantly, with God. Joseph's self-leadership created a power to master his own emotions, and his heart stayed on the Lord and free from grudges, despite the hardships he faced. Joseph shows the principle that forgiving those who hurt us opens a channel of incredible good blessings to the forgiver with absolute peace with God and man.

Jesus Christ's formula: Love, faithfulness, seeking first God's Kingdom.
Jesus' mission was to bring Salvation and deliver a message of Salvation to the whole earth and "whoever believes in Him shall not perish but have everlasting life"(John 3:16). His destination or good success can be measured by His effectiveness and the impact of His message. And Jesus was incredibly successful in those regards and many others. No leader attracted attention and followers as Jesus did in a world that had so many competing beliefs. What was his formula? He left us specific teachings on attitudes for good success. In the Sermon on the Mount, Jesus summarized the blessings of hope in the beatitudes. He said *Blessed are* the poor in spirit, including those who mourn, the meek, those who hunger and thirst for righteousness, the merciful, the pure in heart, the peacemakers, those who are persecuted for righteousness sake, and you when they revile and persecute you for His sake (Matthew 5:3-11). He had comforting words of hope for each group of people addressed.

Jesus' prescription was that to have good success in all the things that matter most; the leader must first seek the kingdom of God and His righteousness, and all the things that matter shall be added to him (Matthews 6:33). His formula was in the passion and content of his message: compassion, love, hope, and equality in the eyes of God in a nonhierarchical classless social system. To seek first the kingdom of God is to follow the wisdom of God's law and receive the reward of everlasting life. His words inspired the courage of a positive faith that if we simply believe in Him and are self-willed to follow and live by the Spirit, nothing is impossible. The followers, young and old, man and woman, leaders and lay people, all found a place and their answers in the message Christ delivered, a message that put humanity above all else. Jesus was authentic and personal, and everything in the world he met and still today, was not. No wonder His message was so riveting and yet comforting that it spread like wide fire. He created a sense of community, churches, and fellowships, which are continuing today to provide Christian groups the training, strength, and support to persevere, in the face of so many challenges in communities that choose to reject the message. To encourage us to follow Him, He modeled a pattern to follow. There is no other good success that can be compared with that of Jesus.

Apostle Paul's formula: Sharpened visions, SMART priorities, focus on the ultimate things first. Apostle Paul was very clear about what his good success was to be—the excellence of the knowledge of Christ Jesus, to gain Christ and be found in Him, to know Him and the power of His resurrection, to share in the fellowship of His sufferings, and to be conformed to His death—that he might attain the resurrection from the dead. His formula was his positive Christ-like habit for success. His formula to know Christ included sharpening his focus by being willing to let go of nice worldly things that did not matter, discerning what hindered him, discovering what he really wanted and what he needed, and knowing the difference and determining how to get it (12-14) –by forgetting the past with single-minded passion. To gain focus on your good success, you must know your priorities and on what to concentrate: If you have priorities but lack concentration, you will know what to do but will never get it done; If you have concentration but lack priorities, you will see excellence but will not progress towards it. To know your priorities and concentration, you must base your actions on the ultimate thing first by working on yourself (strengths and weakness), your priorities (concentrate on the most important things), working with people that matter in your plan for success, and making sure your objective are at least strategic, measurable, and achievable. To have good success, Apostle Paul taught that you must narrow your focus, set your priorities, avoid priorities of things that matter less, pursue goals toward excellence, ask tough questions, avoid procrastination, and control distractions.

In conclusion, only God is good, and only by His goodness (love and sacrifice) and ways (commandments, statutes, judgments) can success be measured and validated to be eternally good. Hence, the formula for good success is to consistently add to good (God's) ways valid choices (obedience, trust, repentance, confession, courage, resilience, positive attitude, sharpened focus, and the ultimate, love, etc.). Here is it:

**GOOD WAYS + GOOD CHOICES =
GOOD SUCCESS**

CHAPTER 6
DISPLAYING COURAGE–DECISIVENESS

Table 3: Good choices for good success

Leader	Good Choices	Good Success
Isaac	Obedience to God's commandments, statutes, and laws. Self-will, self-regulation, Perseverance	A destiny carrier for God's promises. He watched and followed his father Abraham. He demonstrated a model of self-will and great patience He obeyed God and followed his commands. He became the father of the Jewish nation, fathering Jacob and Esau beginning with Jacob's 12 sons that formed the 12 tribes of Israel.
Moses	Submissive Obedience to God's ways, Trust, True Faith, Intimate walk with God	Delivery of Israel from Bondage: Led the Children of Israel out of slavery from Egypt despite the enormous odds. He led this huge mass of people that contended with God through the desert, kept order, received and delivered the Ten Commandment; brought Israel o the border of their future Promised Land in Canaan.
Joshua	Consistent obedience, resilience, courage, obedience in God's ways	Promised Land: unwavering loyalty and faith in God; he successfully led the people of God out of the desert to conquer their enemies and enter the "Promised Land" of eternity
David	Consistent obedience, trust, confession, repentance, walks in God's ways.	After Good Heart: David's reign established the "Davidic Dynasty" and fulfilled the prophetic vision under which the "messiah" would come. Left a good legacy for his son to follow
Joseph	Obedience to God ,positive attitude (forgiveness, self-mastery, diligence, hard work, faithfulness),	Value of Act of Forgiveness: Joseph trusted God no matter how bad his situation got. He was a skilled, conscientious administrator. He saved not only his own people, but all of Egypt from starvation; he prospered in everything he did
Jesus Christ	Consistent obedience to God, love , faithfulness, seek first God's Kingdom and His righteousness	Salvation and redemption: He lived a sinless life; He laid down his life and paid for the sins of the world for the salvation and the pardon of men to restore fellowship with God, opening the way to eternal life.

Apostle Paul	Consistent emulation of Christ, diligence, sharpened focus, SMART priorities, focus on ultimate things first	Gospel message: planting churches, preaching the gospel, and giving strength and encouragement to early Christians. Paul created a theological framework for understanding Jesus' death and resurrection

Traits of courageous leaders [26]:

1. **Confront reality head-on.** Only by knowing the true current state can you lead your team to a better place!
2. **Seek feedback and listen.** Feedback is not always easy to hear, but it can breathe new life into your relationships and leadership style if you listen and act.
3. **Say what needs to be said.** Having crucial conversations and having the courage to put your opinions on the table, even if they are unpopular.
4. **Encourage push-back.** Encouraging constructive dissent and healthy debate, to reinforce the strength of the team
5. **Take action on performance issues.** Confronting people on issues is hard, which is why so many leaders ignore them until they become a toxic threat to the team or company's performance.
6. **Communicate openly and frequently.** Keep the lines of communication open, even when you don't know all the answers. They also share information instead of hoarding it.
7. **Lead change.** Envision a better way, a valid solution, and a great product; – then approach it with determination and an open mind, knowing that it will be messy and that a mid-course correction may be necessary.
8. **Take decisions and move forward.** Commit to a decision and move ahead. Avoid the crutch of 'analysis paralysis' and make the decision. Forward movement is always better than being stuck in place. Act quickly and decisively when faced with moral issues. When a subordinate does something wrong, a leader must react instantly, with fairness, to the situation at hand.
9. **Give credit to others.** Let go of the need for praise and instead give the credit to those around you.
10. **Hold people (and yourself) accountable.** Expect people to perform and deliver on their commitments, and have the courage

to call them out when they don't follow through. Demonstrate accountability by holding yourself responsible for modeling the behaviors you expect from others and ensuring that dignity and respect are maintained in environments.
11. Be in front of followers. This takes courage. Leadership from the front encapsulates the adage, *never ask a subordinate to do something that you, the leader, wouldn't do.*
12. Demonstrate moral fiber that facilitates courage. Although it can take years to build and is hard-earned, credibility can be lost in a split second if a leader makes a morally wrong choice.

SUMMARY 6
DEVELOPING COURAGE–DECISIVENESS

Before starting this exercise, please read and follow the instruction in the preface of this workbook. Answers to these questions are contained in this chapter. Completion of these exercises after reading the chapter should take 60-90 minutes.

Discovering the Acts of Courage -decisiveness.

1. Give examples of how decisiveness displays courage and evidenced in a leader's ability to take a stand on an issue without fear
2. A sense of quickness to act on issues is an attribute of courage decisiveness. How can taking a stand a direct product of decisiveness? How can Decisive courage be displayed?
3. One key courageous strategy for confronting human performance issues is effective communication. What are some courage-decisiveness strategies you can use?
4. Malachi is a good case study of confronting human performance factors through effective communication that focuses first on connecting to the follower. "Leaders earn the right to change the life of their followers by first affirming their identity and relationship to the leader" [15] (Malachi 1:2-14). What were some of the strategies used in this context

Understanding the Principle of Courage Good Success

1. *If you can see it, you can reach it, but only with the right choices!* Moses proved this principle.
    a. Why did God not allow him to reach his destined good success
2. State the principle of good success. Success is a direct result of your habit, which is shaped by behaviors and choices in life. What is a *success habit?*
3. State the additive law of good success.
4. List six of the twelve traits of courageous leaders [26]:

Practice: A Case Study of Courage for Good Success

Courage-Decisiveness is the ability to readily and openly make tough decisions without fear of your critics on challenging issues, uncomfortable criticism, and opposite opinions.

1. What meaning or lesson can you frame from the experience of reading this chapter?
2. How is decisiveness a characteristic of responsibility?
3. How does the decisiveness display the courage-ability to take a stand on an issue without fear?
4. How do you display courage in confronting daunting human performance factors that take courage?
5. What is a 'good success' What are the four most common success-habits of successful people
5. What was most unique about success and failures of in of Abraham Lincoln's life?
6. How is self-will as an element of self-leadership the greatest mentor to turn failure into credible success?.
7. The Bible differentiates success with an internal value from good success with eternal value. How is *good success the achievement of something that is of eternal value to God.*
8. : Is there a rule or principle for good success that can be consistently applied with some guaranteed result in all areas of our lives?.
9. List some examples of good success. How can good success lead to other greater success? How can success in practicing

forgiveness, whereby you release someone that hurts you, lead to prosperity and good blessings from God?
10. The Formula for Good Success: What are the key good choice elements of formula of good success for the following Biblical leaders :

Leader	Good Choices	Good Success
Isaac,		
Moses,		
Joshua,		
Joseph,		
Daniel,		
Nehemiah,		
Paul,		
Jesus Christ		

11. Why did Moses fail to reach his destined success for the Promised Land; he saw the Promised Land but could not go in. Why?

Topic Index

About This Book, 22
authentic, 24, 26
authentic leadership, 37
Authentic Leadership, 45
Authenticity, 43
Bravery Model for Good Success, 97
Case
of overcoming fear, 71, 74
Characteristics of Servant Leadership
Courage -Attribute, 54, 62
Comfort, 41
commitment, 19, 25
communication
types of, 30
Communication, 30
Comparisons
with other works, 40
Compassion, 28
Courage-bravery, 65, 73
Courage-decisiveness, 89, 109
Courage-Self-Will, 85
Courage-Strength, 62, 77, 81
credibility, 48
Empathy-attribute, 28
forgive, 69
Formula for good success, 98, 111
Functional Definitions, 35
giving, 86, 104, 108
Good Success
Apostle Paul's formula, 106
Jesus Christ's formula, 105
Joseph's formula, 104
Joshua's formula, 102
King David's formula, 103
Good Success
Moses Formula, 100
Increase the presence of the Lord, 67, 74
Initiative
definition of, 29
inside-out, 46
Joshua, 19
law of, 42
LEADER, 28
Leader as Servant Leadership, 42
definition, 25

Leader First., 23
Leader-as-Servant Leadership, 23
leader-servant's affection-attribute
definition, 48
leadership, 25
Leadership Attributes, 43
Leadership Inner Value system, 25
Learning to be Courageous, 60, 62
Model, 23
moral capital, 87
Moses, 19
Navigation-attribute, 48
Personal Outward Authenticity, 47
Principle of Servant Leadership
Courage -Attribute, 58
process, 25
self-awareness, 95
Self-will, 96
Servant, 23, 24
sources of fear, 65, 73
Strategies
overcoming fear, 62, 66
Successful leaders
Perseverance, 95
Self-confidence, 95
Self-determination, 95
Successful leaders
Self-will, 94
Teachable Moments to Grow, 87
test
for leader-servant authenticity, 46
of essential elements of personal
 authenticity, 46, 47
The Leadership Persuasion –Attribute
defined, 59, 62
The Leadership Influence-attribute, 41
The Principle of Leadership Empathy-Attribute,
 28
The Principle of Leadership Adaptability
 Attribute, 27
The Principle of Leadership listening-attribute, 30
Traits of courageous leaders, 108, 110
Trust, 66, 74
Walking with God, 80, 81
overcoming fear, 66, 73

REFERENCES

[1]Greenleaf, R. (1970). *The Servant as Leader,* Indianapolis: The Robert K. Greenleaf Center

[2]Spears, L. (1996*).* *"Reflections on Robert K. Greenleaf and servant-leadership."* Leadership & Organization Development Journal, 17(7), 33-35

[3]Russell, R.F. (2001). "The role of values in servant leadership." *Leadership & Organization Development Journal,* 22(2), 76-83

[4]Russell, R.F., and Stone, A.G. (2002). "A review of servant leadership attributes: developing a practical model." *Leadership & Organization Development Journal,* 23(3), 145-15

[5]Terry. R. W (1993*). Authentic Leadership: Courage In Action,* San Francisco, CA ,Jossey-Bass

[6]George, B (2003). *Authentic Leadership: Rediscovering the Secrets to Creating Lasting Value.* San Francisco, CA, Jossey-Bass

[7]Shamir, B. & Eilam, G. (2005). "What's your story? Toward a life-story approach to authentic leadership." Leadership Quarterly, 16, 395–418.

[8]Anderson, GL (2009). Advocacy Leadership: Toward a Post-Reform Agenda in Education, Routledge, New York, 41

[9]Yacobi, B.G. *"Elements of Human Authenticity."* http://www.philosophytogo.org /wordpress/?p=1945, Retrieved, July 15, 2012

[10]George, B (2003). *Authentic Leadership: Rediscovering the Secrets to Creating Lasting Value,* San Francisco, CA, Jossey-Bass

[11]Wosu, SN (2014), *Leader as Servant Leadership Model,* Xulon Press

[12]RosaParks, https://www.history.com/topics/black-history/rosa-parks

[13]Nelson Mandela (1994), *Long walk to Freedom,* Little, Brown and Company, New York].

[14]Galileo_Galilei, https://en.wikipedia.org/wiki/Galileo_Galilei

[15]Obama;http://www.commentarymagazine.com/2012/03/13/biden-obama-risked-reelection-to-kill-bin-laden/

[16] Kenexa High Performance Institute (2011), "Trust Matters: New Links to Employee Retention and Well-being." WorkTrend Report, 2011/2012 http://www.kenexa.com/Portals/0/Downloads/KHPI%20Papers/KHPI%20WorkTrends%20Report%20-%20Trust%20Matters.pdf

[17] Winston Churchill, http://www.winstonchurchill.org/.

[18] History Place, "Alicoln" http://www.historyplace.com/lincoln/index.html

[19] Henry S. Truman, http://www.whitehouse.gov/about/presidents/HarrySTruman. Retrieved August 12, 2014

[20] Albert Einstein Biography, http://www.nobelprize.org/nobel_prizes/physics/laureates/1921/einstein-bio.html.

[21] Isaac Newton's Life, http://www.newton.ac.uk/newtlife.html.

[22] The life of Henry Ford, http://www.hfmgv.org/exhibits/hf/

[23] Gerald Beals, "The Biography of Thomas Edison, "http://www.thomasedison.com/biography.html

[24] Bill Gates, http://en.wikipedia.org/wiki/Bill_Gates

[25] Oprah Winfrey, Wikipedia, http://en.wikipedia.org/wiki/Oprah_Winfrey.

[26] Thorlin, Fred (April 2000). Fred Thorlin: The Big Boss at Atari Program Exchange. Interview with Kevin Savetz. Atari archives. http://www.atariarchives.org/APX/thorlininterview.php. Retrieved December 6, 2016

www.ingramcontent.com/pod-product-compliance
Lightning Source LLC
LaVergne TN
LVHW051217070526
838200LV00063B/4932